Festiniog
Railway
In Camera
One Hundred
Years 1871-1971

by M.J.Stretton

Copyright: Challenger Publications & M.J.Stretton
First published in the United Kingdom
by Challenger Publications 1999
ISBN 1 899624 40 6

Challenger Publications, Penistone, S. Yorkshire.
Printed and bound by Seddon Printers, Moor Lane, Bolton,
Greater Manchester.

CHALLENGER PUBLICATIONS

A small sign that says so much! Few could have predicted the sheer magnitude of the achievements by successive groups of staff, supporters and volunteers after the 'mad' decision was taken in the early 1950s to rebuild the FR. Note the 'laid back' approach to exhortation in those days - "Are you <u>interested</u>...."! - and the gentle plea at the foot. How much weight would such a request carry today? *Central Electric Authority.*

Dedication

This book is respectfully dedicated to the memory of Michael Seymour, who died of cancer on 28th February 1999. His stewardship of the railway's priceless heritage will be valued beyond measure by future historians.

Acknowledgements

As with any project of this sort, the finished product is the result of help and co-operation from a number of individuals and organisations - this book is no different. There are too many to mention all by name, but one must rank for especial thanks - Adrian Gray. Secretary of the Festiniog Railway Heritage Group, he has more recently assumed the mantle of Hon. Archivist to the Railway, following the decline in health of Michael Seymour. Without Adrian's ever-willing patience, courtesy, enthusiasm, help and encouragement - as well as gentle pointers when I was veering down an errant path - the book would have been much the poorer, both in content and accuracy. His time in proof-reading when incredibly busy elsewhere, and his constructive comments, cannot easily be repaid.

Photographers, too, are essential people and those whose material has been used within these pages are hereby offered my profuse thanks, for their skills, far-sightedness and permission to use the products of their labours. All are acknowledged, but particular thanks go to Robin Butterell, Hugh Ballantyne, Gerald Adams, Peter Johnson, Jon Marsh, Martin Cook, Peter Treloar, Peter Gray and Sydney Leleux for their material and their trust.

Sadly, during the preparation of this book, the above-mentioned Mike Seymour died. President of the Heritage Group, it is in no small part due to him that I became involved with and a supporter of the FR. Honorary Archivist to the Railway virtually since its inception in the mid-Fifties, his patience and care in answering and guiding this ignoramus towards the Holy Grail, in my early years of knowing him, was appreciated more than he ever knew. I found him a gentleman in the true sense and he and his knowledge will be sorely missed. I make no excuses, therefore, for dedicating this book to him.

Finally, thanks go, as ever, to my long-suffering wife Judi, herself a lover of the FR (which helps!); to my daughter Tammy, for becoming involved as a volunteer; to Eileen and Neil Clayton for nurturing and encouraging her involvement; to the FR itself for providing both photographic opportunities and immense enjoyment to myself and many thousands more; and to John Hooper of Challenger for being almost as enthusiastic about this project as myself. Without you all I could not have done it!

Front cover - top.
Although construction of the Festiniog Railway took place from both ends, the 'first sod' was cut at Creuau, a point much nearer half-way. In 1871, double-Fairlie LITTLE WONDER stands on Creuau Bank, attempting to show the reality of its name, with an incredibly long rake of rolling stock. The long tail of the train is where Tan-y-Bwlch station now stands. *MJS collection.*

Front cover - bottom.
One hundred years later and on the 'new' FR, double-Fairlies still hold sway. 1886-vintage EARL OF MERIONETH climbs towards the station stop at Dduallt with an afternoon 'Up' train in the summer of 1971. Displaying the final development of the design, as perpetuated by the original company, and originally named LIVINGSTON THOMPSON, the locomotive was withdrawn at the end of the 1971 season and is now on long term loan to the National Railway Museum at York. *John Edgington.*

Rear cover.
Over the ten decades covered by this book, the Tan-y-Bwlch site has seen much change and development. A strategic place throughout its existence, especially as a crossing point for 'Up' and 'Down' trains, this importance has not diminished as the restored railway has once more forged its way northwards. In the summer of 1971, EARL OF MERIONETH enters the station with a Porthmadog-Dduallt service. The area to the left is now open to the public, with picnic tables from which to view the trains. *John Edgington.*

Introduction

We are lucky to be able to enjoy the Ffestiniog Railway. Going into the new Millennium, it is over 160 years since the railway first saw the light of day and it is by happy accident that it is still here. This is not to denigrate the Herculean efforts made by many hundreds of people over the past half century, but without such accidents they would have been thwarted.

The history of the FR is a long convoluted story and one of overcoming immense obstacles, both physical and otherwise. The actual story has been told in other places in great detail and it is not my intention in this volume to do other than to sketch in some pertinent and/or interesting pointers to the greater canvas. As will be seen from Chapter One, the story goes back nearly two hundred years to the vision and drive of one man. Without him, neither the railway nor the area of North Wales around Porthmadog, since enjoyed by millions of tourists, would have existed as we know them. The tale is a fascinating and engrossing one and I urge anyone who has visited even for one day, to explore further, both in text and on the ground.

In this book, I have attempted to put together a selection of views of the railway's history. These are not inclusive by any manner of means, but are merely signposts to what there was and is. The pictorial period covered is one hundred years, from 1871 to 1971. This might seem somewhat arbitrary, seeing that the railway was 'born' in 1836 and saw steam for the first time in 1863, but - again by happy accident! - 1871 is the date of the earliest photograph used, and 1971 neatly brings us to the end of a particularly frenetic period on the restored railway in the 1960s; to a period of some consolidation before the next leap forward, and to a harbinger of that progress with the fitting of oil-firing to BLANCHE in 1971. The railway was constructed to move slate from Blaenau Ffestiniog to Portmadoc and the first chapter of the book reflects this journey. Chapters Two and Three then move chronologically from 1951 to 1971, looking at two decades of restoration of the railway, from uncertain beginnings to substantial achievements.

The written text, likewise, offers pieces of the jigsaw, to both show some of the story and to whet the reader's appetite (hopefully!) to learn more, although I have gone back further than 1871 for completeness and continuity. Other books on the railway will repay investigation and past volumes of the Society's magazine can also be obtained from appropriate sources. These latter, especially, show some of the traumas endured in the magnificent and majestic progress northwards from Porthmadog in the mid-Fifties.

Volunteers have always been - and still are - a vital source of manpower on the FR. The future will be no different and I hope that many reading this book will be fired (if you will excuse the pun) to add their names to the long list of past (and present) 'heroes'. But merely by buying this book, you have supported the railway and I thank you!

Finally, there are still images crying out for publication and, hopefully, many will be included in a second volume. If, however, you have photographs and/or memorabilia that have not been published, I would be very interested in seeing them (especially older views). Initial contact can be made through the publishers and your precious material will be well cared for. I look forward to hearing from you!

John Stretton
March 1999

Opposite. **It is true to say that without, over the years, a continuing band of dedicated, far-sighted, talented and enthusiastic individuals, the Ffestiniog Railway would not be the remarkable outfit that it is today. In the early years, one man had as much drive and influence as any other. That man was Allan Garraway and he is seen here as driver of PRINCE in the summer of 1957. Waiting to take his train forward from Harbour station in Portmadoc, he takes time out to share conversation with fireman David Ronald and another, off-duty, volunteer, David Rouse.** *Norman Keen.*

As mentioned elsewhere, the raison d'être of the Festiniog Railway was slate and its transhipment from the quarries above Blaenau Ffestiniog to Portmadoc. Produce from the Maenofferen and Votty & Bowydd Quarries was brought down from the mining operations to the town by steep inclines, the slate then being marshalled at Duffws station yard before travelling south-west to the port. In 1906, WELSH PONY stands at the head of a rake of empty slate wagons, preparing them for hauling up the rope-controlled incline to Maenofferen, out of sight to the left. The fact that passenger services are still running into Duffws can be judged by the presence of bogie luggage van No.3, seen just to the left of the luggage cart on the platform, right. *N.Kerr, Peter Johnson collection.*

As might be imagined, with extensive quarrying around the town, there was need for hundreds of mine workers and many of these travelled to and from the operations, although not daily, via the FR. To accommodate them, the railway was required to provide a number of 'quarrymen's coaches' and a long rake of them can be seen here, behind a much earlier view of WELSH PONY. Again undated, but undoubtedly in Victorian days and probably around the 1870s, this shot shows the England locomotive in original condition, before its rebuild in 1890. Compare with the above photograph for differences and note that the provision of a proper cab, although improving conditions for the footplate crew in inclement weather, did rather restrict their movements. *Peter Johnson collection.*

After the introduction of double-Fairlies on the FR in 1879, they took over the lion's share of passenger operations up to Duffws, 720ft. above sea level. In a scene from around the turn of the century, double-Fairlie JAMES SPOONER poses for the photographer by the capacious goods shed, with crew and station staff in attendance and quarry spoil heaps prominent in the background. *Percy Pike collection.*

Chapter One:
Pre-preservation

The story of the Festiniog Railway (with one 'F' as mistakenly registered by an English management) is inextricably linked with slate, but the story goes back beyond the actual laying of rails.

The years of the eighteenth century were dark days indeed for the inhabitants of many parts of our small island, but perhaps none more so than the mountainous region of Snowdonia, where the largely peasant people eked out a hand-to-mouth living. With much of the area isolated and often cut-off in the inclement winter weather, neither was there any money with which to enrich the lives of the thousands involved in the cottage industry of spinning and weaving the fleece of the hundreds of thousands of Welsh sheep, or much will to even try. To change the situation, as was being done ever more frequently in England, needed people with vision and wealth. Enter William Alexander Madocks.

Born the third son of an eminent and wealthy English society family, who had been North Wales landed gentry for generations, he inherited little when his father died, the bulk of the estate going to his elder brother. Although comfortable within his society, he had his own views and these were espoused and employed as Member of Parliament for Boston, Lincolnshire. Like many in his family and their associates, he had a love of the 'delightful picturesque' North Wales scenery, but rather than merely appreciate this during the pleasant summer months, he had a burning desire to change the status quo. He wanted to open up the area, to address some of the poverty surrounding the family estates. This idea was not always looked upon favourably by those involved in North Wales, but he was undaunted.

Despite the relative paucity of his own fortune, he had visions built of eighteenth century amateurism, which either did not recognise or simply overlooked problems and obstacles to the completion of these grand ideas. Add to this that the execution of early schemes was done at arms length, by correspondence with one John Williams - a garden-boy before employment by Madocks - and the mind boggles! But, to our story.

In 1798, long desperate for some land of his own after graduation from Oxford, his mother advanced him his legacy, to buy land, poor by any standards, on the edge of the Traeth Mawr estuary separating the counties of Caernarvon and Merioneth. At high tide the estuary flooded whole swathes of land around what we now know as Tremadog and Porthmadog and his first plan was to stem some of this expanse by constructing an embankment to enclose some 1,000 acres of marshland bordering his small estate. Around the same time the Act of Union between England and Ireland was ratified and Madocks had ideas of capitalising on this.

Holyhead was not yet developed, so Porthdinllaen, an anchorage on the western coastline of Caernarvonshire would, if linked to Dublin, give the shortest route to London and, for Madocks, provide a lucrative trade from the mail and stage coaches literally passing his door. At one stroke it would open up the area to some degree of prosperity and would give Madocks the encouragement and wherewithal to progress to greater schemes. His vision given free rein, the town of Tre Madoc was conceived and Town it was in his mind from the first; no mere village this! For example, the town hall was constructed in grand style, dramatically and theatrically positioned under the lee of the cliff that had previously stood on the edge of the estuary, facing what he grandly called London Street. The other main approach road was Dublin Street, to reinforce his idea. But there was one great obstacle to this grand scheme - that very same Traeth Mawr estuary, at the point where the Afon Glaslyn met the Irish Sea.

William Madocks was not the first to have the idea of damming the estuary. By 1806 he was virtually obsessed with the idea but was faced, as were others before him, with the problem of how to build a mile-long dam able to withstand the vagaries and pressures of weather, the extreme rise and fall of the tide and, to face those forces during construction. Initially all seemed set fair, with eldest brother John financing the Bill through Parliament and James Creassy, the engineer of the 1800 embankment, on board to oversee the works. Dramatically, however, within days of the Bill coming to the Commons John was dead, with Creassy following shortly thereafter! Madocks was on his own.

As if emulating Nelson, with his 'blind eye' turned to the resultant problems, Madocks ploughed on regardless. Again John Williams was employed as agent and again instructions were given by post, as Madocks needs must spend time in London, seeing his Bill through Parliament. It took three years to bridge the gap and four days were set aside in September 1811 to enjoy the celebrations, which were to include plays, balls, races, an Eisteddfod and an ox-roasting at the mid-point of the embankment. The sense of disbelief and desolation when a combination of a south westerly gale and an unusually high tide breached the new structure near that mid-point shortly afterward, can only be imagined. A veritable army of men and horses battled the elements to restore matters. It was eventually fixed 'at enormous cost'. Many a man would have quit at this point, but not Madocks.

Facing bankruptcy, (unable to even afford the coach fare home from London!), and crippled with gout, he was undeterred. He never stopped thinking of how to overcome his fate and somewhat prophetically wrote to John Williams, regarding his plans, "If I can only give them birth, shape and substance before I die, they will work their own way to prosperity." His mind was encompassing harbour, railroad, road to Harlech, a clay-burning system for improving agriculture locally, and a scheme for attracting sea-bathers! Truly he was a visionary, but slowly others too were appreciating the area and its potential.

Within ten years of the above disaster, many other eyes had turned towards North Wales. Madocks never ceased to badger John Williams with his instructions, sometimes down to the smallest detail and with an urgency derived of failing health and anxiety not to lose his goal. Perhaps his greatest dream was to see the wealth of the slate quarries around Blaenau Ffestiniog flow to his newly built port by Traeth Mawr, modestly called Port Madoc. He was concerned that the importance of this undertaking was fully understood, but sadly,

Two views of LITTLE GIANT at Duffws in 1929. Built in 1867, along with WELSH PONY, LITTLE GIANT received its enclosed cab when reboilered in 1887. Its tank, chimney and smokebox were all replaced, but the engine did not last as long as some of its 'siblings', being withdrawn in 1932, its firebox condemned. *(top)* **A two-coach passenger service arriving in typical Blaenau Ffestiniog weather. Five quarrymen's coaches stand in the siding, right, whilst a porter and young lad, hands in pockets, watch the last few yards of the climb.** *(below)* **LITTLE GIANT rests after its exertions. Passengers have all alighted, leaving doors of coach No.20 open, whilst behind, bogie brake van No.3 is about to receive a milk churn.** *Both Dr.Jack Hollick, Adrian Vaughan collection.*

Without his vision and legacy, we would not have had the Ffestiniog Railway we do today. 1814 saw the completion of the embankment across the estuary that is now universally known as 'The Cob'. The town of Port Madoc was literally born within a decade - it did not exist at all in 1800!

The tramway that eventually became the railway we know today, owed its creation to the need of Samuel Holland, owner of Rhiwbryfdir quarry in Blaenau Ffestiniog. With a growing demand for his slate from the rapidly expanding English towns, mushrooming in response to the demands of the Industrial Revolution, he was desirous of moving his produce quickly and cheaply. The costly, laborious, time-consuming and potentially unsuccessful chain of mule-pack, horse-drawn wagons, small river craft and, finally, open-water craft was just not acceptable. The last transfer, in mid-estuary, was also restricted by weather and tide. Therefore, with a secure anchorage scoured out by the pent-up Afon Glaslyn from behind the Cob, conditions were ripe for alternative schemes. With the Cob, harbour and town all completed by 1824, two schemes for a railway from the quarries around Blaenau Ffestiniog to Portmadoc were proposed.

he was to die - in 1828, on his way home from Naples - eight years before the railway and the prosperity that it brought to the region saw the light of day. Soon, Welsh slate was roofing the world and all manner of commodities flowed into Port Madoc, immeasurably enhancing the livelihoods of the locals. By 1845, the Festiniog Railway handled 43,000 tons of slate for export and in the port, some 29,000 tons of shipping was required to handle the cargoes.

Neither succeeded as put to Parliament and other schemes floated in the ensuing five years also failed. It was in 1829 that Holland met Henry Archer, an Irishman interested in local railways, and the rest is history.

The Act of Parliament, sanctioning the Festiniog Railway, came on 23rd May 1832, with construction moving from both ends but launched at Creuau, near what is now the site of Tan-y-Bwlch station, on 26th February 1833. Archer was the

A post-war view depicting the quarry lines after the station was closed, on December 1931, rails lifted and a wall built to separate the two sides of the site. Originally opened in 1866, Duffws was the sole northern terminus from 1870 until closure, apart from a brief hiatus of 'mini closure' (to passengers) in 1923/4. On 23rd July 1951 the sun shines brightly, clearly showing the incline's steep gradient up to Votty & Bowydd (Oakeley from 1933) and, left, abandoned wagons. The Maenofferen line curves to the left just past the wagons. *R.C.Riley, Peter Johnson collection.*

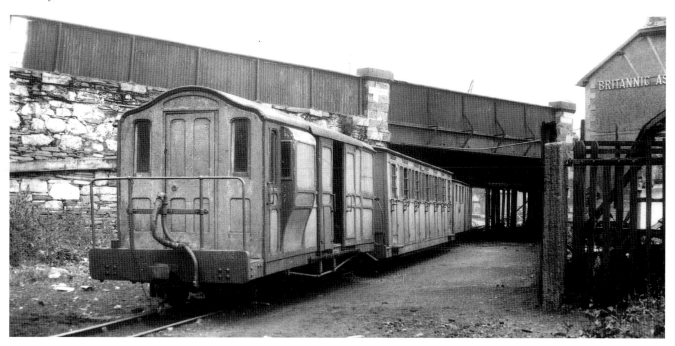

Non-slate stock on the FR was a mixture of purely passenger coaches and more utilitarian units. The Railway was one of the earliest to employ bogie coaches, but despite the success of these, most non-passenger stock remained non-bogie. However, three bogie brake vans were built at Boston Lodge between 1873 and 1876, on timber underframes and with curly roofs. As well as containing space for baggage, they all originally also had a dog compartment! Only two survived to the closure of the railway in 1946, Nos.2 and 3. The former had been rebuilt with standard roof outline by then and, now as No.10, survives on the present FR. No.3, sadly, though in original condition, rotted too far for restoration to be attempted. In happier times, between the wars, No.3 is seen at the end of a short rake underneath Queen's Bridge, with one of those early coaches next to it and the platform of Duffws station just visible beyond. *Peter Johnson collection.*

Originally double track - until 1932 - the route southwards from Duffws ran into a facility shared with the Great Western, later known as Blaenau Ffestiniog Central station. In this view, looking back towards Duffws in 1887, as well as the tall GWR somersault signal, notice the two imposing gantries on the FR line just short of Queen's Bridge. The importance to Blaenau Ffestiniog of slate traffic was reflected in the railway presence, with this being just one of five terminal stations in the town over the years - three FR, one GWR and one LNWR/LMS. Some of the expanse of railway land at this point in the town can be judged from the goods shed to the right, which in turn had extensive slate sidings beyond it. Looking at the site today, with standard and narrow gauge re-aligned and land built on up to the area of the goods shed, it is almost impossible to visualise the past layout. Only the Queen's Hotel and the house extreme left remain today! *R.H.Bleasdale, FR Archives.*

fund-raiser, with others, including the influential James Spooner, seeing to the building and the railway finally opened for business on 20th April 1836. Although the Act did not specify either gauge or mode of transport, the railway was laid to 1'11½", to match lines already in the quarries and was initially horse-worked up the 13-mile climb to Blaenau Ffestiniog, some 700ft. above sea level. The downward journey was by gravity, as the line was brilliantly constructed on a continuously falling gradient, apart from two rope-operated inclines over slopes of the Moelwyn mountains. There was widespread doubt that the line could be built, in view of the terrain and it was fortunate that the engineers settled on so narrow a gauge, rather than the 3ft. version that had originally run on the Cob!

Success was not immediate - it took time for some of the quarry owners to recognise the advantages of the railway but once they had, it was assured. By 1842, the two inclines at Moelwyn had been 'sidelined' by the tunnel and there was no hindrance to the rapid growth in slate traffic.

Charles Easton Spooner, Engineer and Secretary to the Festiniog Railway Co., was a man of vision who recognised the potential for the Festiniog as a passenger carrying railway. To convert the idea to practice, he would have to introduce

steam locomotives, to keep a realistic schedule, but, in the late 1850s, despite advances made in the previous thirty years of steam railways, 1'11½" narrow gauge locomotives did not exist. Even the great Robert Stephenson declared the idea impossible, the debate of the day being between Stephenson's 4' 8½" and Brunel's 7' 'Broad' gauges. Undaunted, Spooner did not give up. Traffic in slate was still growing, and horse and gravity working was fast approaching the limit of the line's capacity.

As the 1860s dawned, the FR began thinking about Parliamentary powers to double the line, to keep up with customers' demands. This course would have been enormously expensive so, in 1861, Spooner asked locomotive builders to submit designs and tenders for suitable locomotives.

Solutions offered were very varied. In the end, a contract was awarded to George England & Co. of London for three locomotives. Of 0-4-0 wheel-arrangement, the first pair, THE PRINCESS and MOUNTAINEER - with side tanks and open cabs - arrived in Wales in 1863. They were not an instant success. The design faults could not be laid entirely at George England's door, however, and to appease him for the extra work in putting matters right, the order was increased to four

Another view of the joint Central station, opened in 1883, this time from the footbridge, on Tuesday, 22nd January 1946. By comparison with the above view, many changes become apparent. A new point has been added on the FR route, allowing locomotives to run round at the GWR platform, in conjunction with the 1932 alterations to the approach to the now-closed Duffws station; the FR signal brackets have gone; the flower beds and gas lamps have vanished from the GWR platform, as has the tall signal post; trees have grown up, left; and the Queens' Hotel has lost its side wall sign. Although the presence of coaching stock on the standard gauge gives the appearance of healthy traffic, the area does not have the appeal of the older shot above and it is not just the time of year creating this feel. The only sign of movement, is the activity surrounding PRINCESS, shunting slate wagons on the FR tracks. *Robin Butterell.*

A short time later and PRINCESS has collected a brakevan and coupled up to its train of empty slate wagons. Standing in the shared platform, the fireman and the photographer's sister pose for their portrait, before the train moves westwards to the exchange sidings. It would be interesting to know what was in the sack on PRINCESS' tender! *Robin Butterell.*

A brief look at the exchange sidings at the east, Great Western end of Blaenau Ffestiniog. Prominent on Wednesday, 20th November 1946, is a special 14 Ton wagon used by the GWR between the town and Manod quarries, to transport narrow gauge wagons. Numbered 25020, it was, at this date, one of a pair and carried a maximum of eight of the four-wheeled wagons, on specially laid tracks. *Robin Butterell.*

locomotives: THE PRINCE and PALMERSTON, to the modified design, arrived shortly afterwards.

Slate traffic continued to grow and this, combined with the beginning of a passenger service on 6th January 1865, led to two more similar, but slightly larger locomotives - WELSH PONY and LITTLE GIANT - being built in 1867. Slate tonnage more than doubled, from 51,000 in 1860 to 112,000 in 1868 and line capacity was close to being breached again. The previously considered doubling was authorised by the Festiniog Railway Act of 1869 but was rendered unnecessary by a remarkable addition to the locomotive stock.

In 1864, Robert Francis Fairlie had been granted a patent on a double-boiler, double-bogie articulated locomotive. The FR accepted an offer from George England & Co. to build one of these machines, at a cost of £1,600 and it arrived in 1869. Again, the rest is history.

The aptly-named LITTLE WONDER - Fairlie was not slow at blowing his own trumpet - proved itself capable of more than the combined work of a pair of the 0-4-0s. Spooner, equally publicity conscious, and Fairlie organised demonstrations of LITTLE WONDER's capabilities, attracting international audiences with delegations coming from as far away as Russia. These visits influenced railway development in many parts of the world, by demonstrating the suitability of the narrow gauge for secondary routes or those in difficult terrain and the ability of Fairlies, or other articulated types, to increase the capacity of lines of this type.

In 1872 a heavier double-engine, JAMES SPOONER arrived, designed by George Percival Spooner, Charles' son. Meeting the need for an intermediate engine, a single-Fairlie TALIESIN, effectively half a JAMES SPOONER, was obtained in 1876. The railway then entered a period of considerable

success. Several half-year dividends as high as 5% were paid, a level unheard of for mainline railway companies which, naturally, drew attention to the FR's lucrative traffic. Clouds were gathering.

Various schemes were mooted, lost or amended, but competition of a fashion did come with the eventual standard gauge opening to Blaenau Ffestiniog by two railways - the Great Western from Bala in 1882 (converting the existing narrow gauge tracks of the Festiniog & Blaenau Railway) and the London & North Western in 1879 from Bettws-y-Coed. Also, from 1867, there had been threat and potential loss of trade to the Aberystwyth & Welsh Coast Railway, later becoming part of the Cambrian Coast Railway. These competitors had their impact, however, along with changing fortunes and fashions elsewhere, to the extent that tonnage on the FR slumped from a peak of 139,000 in 1897 to just 9,000 in 1945, the last full year of operation. Dividends also fell from 10% in 1882 to Nil in 1906. On the locomotive front, however, with the combination of passengers and freight, things were much more positive.

Boston Lodge Works had been founded by Madocks in 1807, in the quarry from which materials had been dug at the east end of the Cob, to maintain the wagons and horses used in its construction. When the railway was built, the facilities were taken over and developed in parallel with the fortunes of the line. In 1879, the Works took a step towards immortality by building the railway's first in-house locomotive, double-Fairlie MERDDIN EMRYS, again designed by Spooner. In the same year, MOUNTAINEER, one of the two original 1863 0-4-0s and the railway's initial No.1, was withdrawn, 'worn out and unroadworthy'. LITTLE WONDER was also reaching the end of its life by this stage and, in 1882 plans were laid for

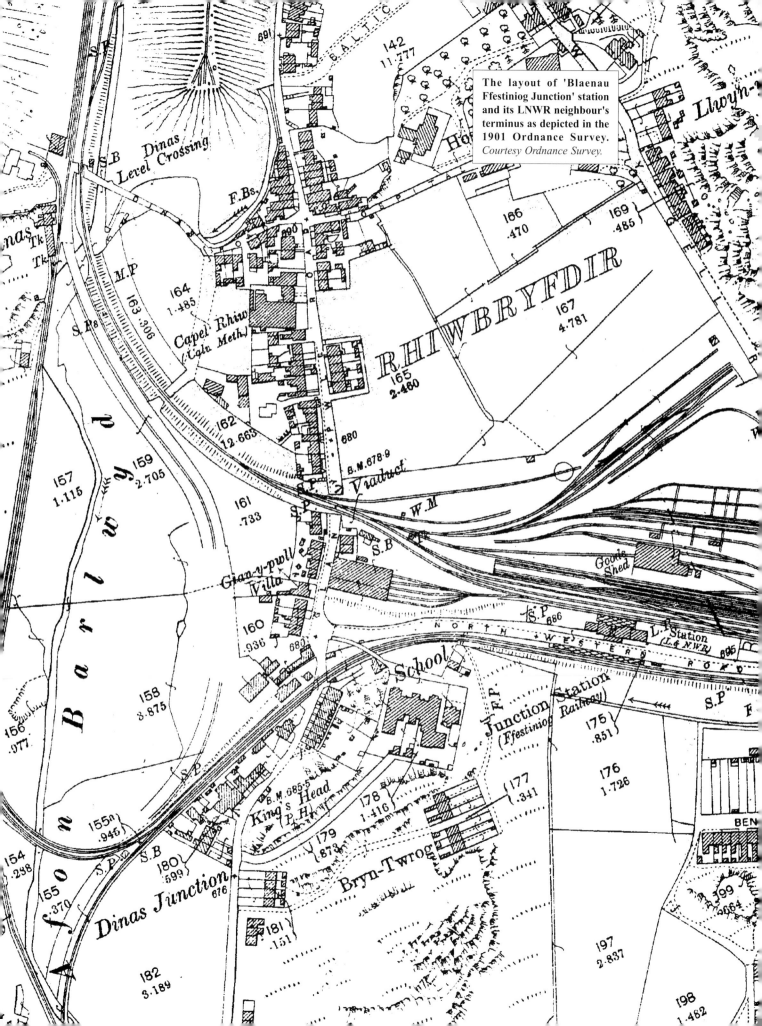

The layout of 'Blaenau Ffestiniog Junction' station and its LNWR neighbour's terminus as depicted in the 1901 Ordnance Survey. *Courtesy Ordnance Survey.*

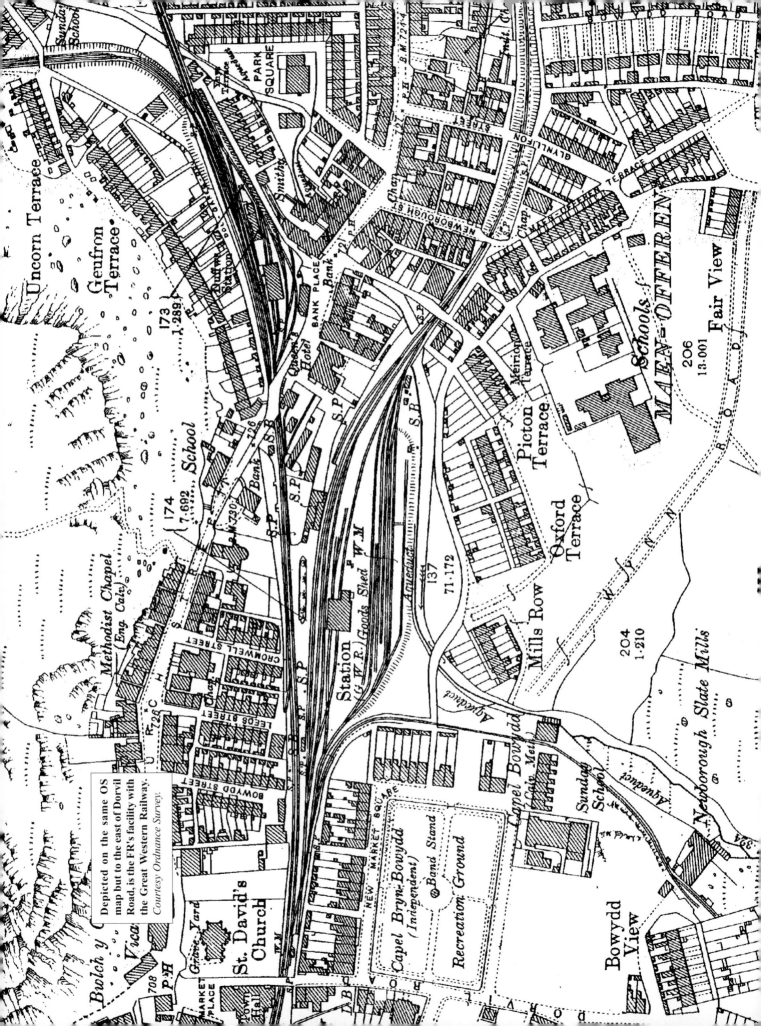

Depicted on the same OS map but to the east of Dorvil Road, is the FR's facility with the Great Western Railway. *Courtesy Ordnance Survey.*

Still in 1946, on 22nd January, PRINCESS prepares to head under the road bridge and enter the exchange yard by the LMS station. With wagons now fore and aft, driver and fireman are keen to be recorded on film, as is the gentleman, presumably the train's guard, on the brakevan. *Robin Butterell.*

a replacement. Virtually a clone of MERDDIN EMRYS, LIVINGSTON THOMPSON was outshopped by Boston Lodge in 1886.

To properly accommodate passengers, and provide offices suitable to a railway of international reputation, Harbour station was rebuilt as a substantial, two-storey, stone building during 1878. From here to 1939, when the railway closed for the duration of the War, operations largely settled into a daily routine, with changes coming with the needs of traffic, running repairs, etc. to the locomotives and reactions to internal and external conditions and influences. The sole single-Fairlie TALIESIN, despite its uniqueness to the FR, seemed to receive no special favours and after around fifty years work, expenditure on the boiler especially was deemed 'un-economic' and the locomotive laid aside, officially being withdrawn in 1931. Almost with indecent haste, the name was transferred to LIVINGSTON THOMPSON, thereby creating conditions for some confusion in later years.

In this period, 1923 was perhaps the most memorable year as Col. H.F.Stephens became railway Engineer, Duffws station closed to passengers (for two years) and the FR became physically associated with the Welsh Highland Railway, by way of a connection laid from Harbour station to the ex-Croesor Tramway route through the town. Through running between Harbour station and Dinas Junction on the new WHR only lasted for two years, however, with the FR thereafter only operating locomotives to Beddgelert.

After the outbreak of War in 1939, only a limited working week for freight purposes ensued, with full gravity work being suspended in 1940. Not suprisingly, slate tonnage halved between 1939/40 and never recovered. The last slate train

ran on 1st August 1946, after which time the line from Duffws to the LMS exchange sidings was leased to Oakeley Quarries. The remaining employees had been given no warning of the closure and as their services were summarily dispensed with, literally overnight, they 'downed tools' and walked away. Thus, like a veritable *Marie Celeste* or a railway version of Miss Haversham in Dickens' *Great Expectations*, the railway sat, gathering cobwebs and gently decaying or disappearing under vegetation, until the preservationists came on the scene.

But even here the story refused to be brought to a close. By law the railway could not merely be abandoned. As the original Act of 1832 contained neither clauses nor provision for the business to fail or require closure, the Law required another Act of Parliament to sanction abandonment. Although the Board would have followed this course, they could not finance the necessary proceedings. Income from rents and leases was meagre, insufficient even to cover the salary of the sole remaining employee, Manager, Robert Evans, or the charges on the overdraft at the Bank. Even the creditors could not force the winding up of the Company, without an Act of Parliament. This impasse lasted through to the early 1950s, when the restorers arrived and took charge of things. Had it not been for this legal 'nicety' (as, indeed, with the case of the WHR, which still fights for its life over sixty years after the last train!), again we would not have had the railway we now enjoy. Fate is, in truth, stranger than fiction.

The LNWR terminus was at the other - western - end of Blaenau Ffestiniog. Opened in 1881, at the same time as the FR station, it enjoyed reciprocal relations with its smaller neighbour. As can be seen from this 1887 view of the FR's 'Blaenau Ffestiniog Junction' station (colloquially known as 'Stesion Fain'), travellers were advised that this was a suitable exchange point for Bettws-y-Coed and Llandudno. Obviously a posed shot, with the two station staff members 'at attention', the station, just six years old, is clean and well cared for; England locomotive LITTLE GIANT is 'pre-rebuild' still with an open cab; and the rather grandiose LNWR buildings look to dominate their neighbour, despite their 'temporary' timber-built nature. These buildings burnt down in 1951 and were replaced by British Railways in 1956, but lasting only until 1982, when the current 'joint' station with the FR opened in the heart of the town. *R.H.Bleasdale, FR Archives.*

A comparison of almost identical trains at Stesion Fain, but separated by more than just years. *(middle)* In a superb view from around the turn of the century, the station buildings still look in good order and the train is magnificent. The fireman of a creditably clean double-engine LIVINGSTON THOMPSON, watches the photographer, as the locomotive restarts its six coach 'up' train towards Central station and Duffws. A four-wheeled quarrymen's coach leads two 'small Birminghams', the two original bogie coaches, 15 and 16 and a large bogie brake van. *Peter Treloar collection.(bottom)* Some thirty-odd years later, in August 1935, the same locomotive now renamed TALIESIN pauses with an eight-coach train. The previous era has been changed out of all recognition by a world war and the Great Depression. Cameras are no longer a novelty and the fireman is not interested in the two photographers, both closer to his train than in the previous view. TALIESIN looks decidedly work-weary. The ageing rolling stock - 'small Birminghams' 12 and 13 and a WHR (ex-NWNGR) Ashbury bogie tourist carriage lead the Festiniog Ashbury bogie workmen's coaches 21 and 22 of 1896, identifiable by their sagging bodywork - shows signs of the 1930s 'Rainbow train' livery. The view of the fence at this end of the station is unusual. *Percy Pike collection.*

After opening in 1881, Stesion Fain enjoyed a healthy business but, latterly, suffered a run-down in overall traffic, in line with the rest of the FR, in the late 1930s. Although passenger traffic figures had been holding up well, the slate business was in decline and from 1936 onwards there was short time and fears of closure. This eventually came with the outbreak of hostilities in September 1939 and although the Railway was not officially closed until August 1946, passenger services never restarted after the War and the station lay abandoned. Signs of deterioration and dereliction can be seen from this view on 12th October 1951 and nature is successfully regaining a hold. The left-hand track was truncated in 1932, leaving just the 'main line' to go onwards, but this was finally cut short, just behind the position of the photographer here, in 1962/3, when the new road to Tanygrisiau was constructed. Happily, the magnificent station canopy did not perish, being rescued for use as a football stand in Manod. *Hugh Ballantyne.*

A view looking the other way, back towards the town of Blaenau Ffestiniog. The date is 14th August 1939 and both country and railway are a short month away from World War; as stated above, the railway would not re-open for passenger traffic. In the late afternoon sunshine, the scene is one of peaceful tranquillity, as the intending passengers await their train, totally belying the momentous events about to hit all of them. *Robin Butterell.*

(left) A few moments later from the previous picture and the 5.30 p.m. train for Portmadoc has arrived. Whether required, or undertaken for photographic purposes, the fireman has left No.10, double-Fairlie MERDDIN EMRYS and looks to effect 'running repairs'. Holding an oil can firmly in his grip, he walks resolutely to the front of the locomotive as the driver, Tom Davies poses and grins at the camera. In the background, a young lady crosses the tracks. Seconds later and (below) the oil can contributes to the assurance of poetry in motion! Bogie brake van No.5 heads the complement of coaches. *both Robin Butterell.*

The aforementioned LNWR station stands to the left of this view of the exchange goods sidings, with the Oakeley Quarry spoil tip in the background. The attractive and somewhat ornate design can be appreciated, as can the solid lines of the substantial goods shed. In the late afternoon sun of 14th August 1939, the FR tracks are seen running in to form four sidings on their raised platform, with standard-gauge tracks on either side of this. Passenger coaches stand in the LMS platform, as the locomotive approaches from the far end, having run round its stock and used the turntable. The former LNWR 3-road carriage shed stands in the background behind the carriages in the platform; on its south side stood the 2-road engine shed. Out of use for many years, neither of these two buildings survived into the BR period. *Robin Butterell.*

(page 20) Twelve years later, 23rd July 1951, the elaborate design can be better seen from this angle, but a closer inspection shows some windows boarded up. The ex-FR tracks, which were here used largely for granite chippings, have now been reduced to just one siding and the state of this and the three wagons standing on it all seem to indicate that this end of the operation is no longer in use. In the right-hand distance, dwarfed by that slate scree, ex-LNWR 'Cauliflower' No.28589 shunts a pick-up goods from Llandudno Junction, whilst, left, ex-LNWR observation car No.1501 - here numbered M15841 - stands waiting its next call of duty. Built at Wolverton Works in 1913, it was one of three such coaches that ran at the rear of trains from Llandudno to Blaenau Ffestiniog, lasting until 1958, when they were replaced by DMUs. The third of the trio is now preserved on the Bluebell Railway. Note the tiny signal box at the platform end, and the BR lorry with just a few coal sacks on board. *R.C.Riley.*

(page 21) Swinging through 90°, the buffer stop seen in the foreground above, is now to the left, as on the 23rd July 1951, a R&H petrol 'tractor' shunts empty slate wagons, as a railman walks ahead to change a point. Note the line of point levers, the far one coming precariously close to Llwyn-y-Gell Road. Certainly in the 1990s, this would be considered very dangerous! *R.C.Riley.*

With the arrival of steam traction in 1863, engine sheds were built at both ends of the line, that at the 'top' being located at Dinas, on the western edge of Blaenau Ffestiniog. Slate-built, it was a one road affair, attached onto the end of the station building, with a barracks for lodging-men included. The station closed around 1870 but the shed remained in use until the turn of the century. Locomotive entrance is seen in this view from 1887, looking north towards the FR's original terminus at Rhiwbryfdir, just below the impressive Welsh Slate Co. viaduct seen in the distance. The layout seen here was replaced in 1899 by double track after realignment of the junction at Glan-y-pwll, behind the photographer. To the right of the photograph is the LNWR line, their semaphore signals making an interesting contrast with the FR's archaic disc beyond the station. *R.H.Bleasdale, Roger Griffiths collection*.

By contrast, the replacement shed at Glan-y-Pwll was a stone built, two road structure. Both sheds would accommodate two locomotives - an England engine as Top shunter and very often TALIESIN, whose duty was the first Down passenger train of the day. The shed fell out of use during WWII and was leased to a timber merchant, as seen in this 1947 view. The typical Blaenau weather cannot have done the stocks of timber much good! *Roger Griffiths collection*.

First stop down the line from Blaenau Ffestiniog was just a mile or so away, at Tanygrisiau, 640ft. above sea level. Opened February 1866, it was originally of timber construction, but was rebuilt in brick and stone in 1879, joining Minffordd at that time as being the only intermediate stations of 'substantial' construction. At the time of erection, a number of slate quarries were already connected to the railway locally and Tanygrisiau was an important and busy place. Some of this importance can be judged from this view on 27th May 1951, which five years after cessation of any traffic on the line, still shows the extent of tracks and sidings at this point. Although here looking decidedly down-at-heel in the dull weather, the grandeur of the station is apparent and the smoke drifting from the workers' cottages reveals that these are still occupied. The smaller of the two wagons stands on the wagon turntable that allowed such vehicles access to the side of the goods shed, seen here proudly adorned by the station nameboard. *Peter Johnson collection.*

As originally built, the railway was on a continuous falling gradient from Blaenau Ffestiniog, apart from two inclines that breasted the spur of the Moelwyns mountain range. This greatly hampered daily operations and so a tunnel through this outcrop was built, opening in 1842. On the northern approaches to the tunnel, the alignment occupied a shallow embankment and this can be seen here on 12th October 1951, looking back towards Tanygrisiau. The station site is just out of view on the extreme right. Although twelve years after normal traffic had ended, the formation still looks in good condition. The construction of the power station in 1963 resulted in the valley being flooded and this view is now under the waters of Llyn Ystradau, the embankment only being revealed at low water. The current FR runs on an alignment higher up the hillside to the left of this view. *Hugh Ballantyne.*

(left) The southern end of Moelwyn tunnel in 1887, showing the tunnel keeper. The tunnel was protected by special signals, the first such installations on the FR, in the days before wholesale use of the electric telegraph to prevent Up and Down trains entering at the same time. The post for the signal can be seen to the left of the tunnel mouth and the keeper is guarding his box of equipment. The widening of the formation is a legacy of the horse-drawn and gravity era, when this was a changing point. The previously employed inclines were to the left of this view. *R H Bleasdale, Percy Pike collection.*

(centre) As explained elsewhere, the FR was built for slate traffic and its success was founded on James Spooner's elegant design, which permitted 'down' traffic to exploit the power of gravity. This being free, the railway only had to bear the lesser cost of returning empty wagons to the quarries, a process that, while it could be done by horses, was relatively inexpensive. Factors conspired to eventually require the introduction of steam locomotives, but gravity trains continued to run until the 1920s. Pictured around 1905, the children from Rhoslyn house, Dduallt, watch one such train passing this remote station, the brakemen sitting on their load, ready for action. The house, unconnected with the railway, still watches over the site, but it has been unoccupied for many years. *FR Archives.*

(below) As one of a number of improvements over the years, to overcome problems with a rather sharp curve running round the outside of the crop, the 60-yd Garnedd Tunnel was completed in 1851. Although not of enormous length and the height of rock above not being particularly massive, the opening of the tunnel greatly assisted operations. Its narrow width, however, has ever since been a restriction on exactly what could travel up the line. There has been talk amongst some in the present FR of reinstating the original route; that can just be glimpsed on the extreme right. This would, however, add more curves to the route. Once more, a century after its construction, nature is attempting a recolonisation in the view from 12th November 1952. *Hugh Ballantyne.*

(right) Undoubtedly, the most strategic point between Blaenau Ffestiniog and Portmadoc was Tan-y-Bwlch, just short of six miles from Duffws. Here was space for trains to pass, passengers to join or leave trains, engines to be watered on their 'up' journey and some freight to be handled in the sidings. Approached from the north over the 1830s-constructed Creuau bank - see front cover - the water tower was the first structure to be reached. In the summer of 1938, with steam possibly leaking from a run-down locomotive, MERDDIN EMRYS restarts its northwards journey, watched by walkers and fellow photographers. At this stage, though having been built sixty years earlier, this engine was still relatively fresh in operation, having been fitted in 1934 with a refurbished boiler, but its bogies were well worn and steam joints were always a problem. Note the exclusivity of short trousers! *Ken Weaver.*

(middle) The same train as above is seen just a few moments earlier as, duly refreshed and watched by yet another short-trousered young man, MERDDIN EMRYS awaits the road, the driver looking back for confirmation of the signal. The tranquil nature of the spot at this time can be appreciated from the surroundings. Prior to 1873, there had not been a station here, the previous halt being at nearby Hafod-y-llyn, but this proved to be inappropriate, not least due to the fact that the spot was not road connected. *Ken Weaver.*

(below) An earlier view, 4th August 1925, shows the station area immediately south of the water tower. To the left is the 1873-vintage booking office, which bears an advertising board offering reciprocal facilities with the L&NWR. Two double-Fairlies cross, the down train behind MERDDIN EMRYS ready with its passengers to continue the journey to Portmadoc and its train crew watching the slow progress of the arriving JAMES SPOONER. Note the gas lamp, seat, signal post with arms inside the post, footbridge (unsafe by 1933) and fencing, to the left of the 'up' train. Within ten years all these artefacts disappeared as the site was opened out. *H.G.W.Household, Peter Johnson collection.*

(above) In the 1930s, much was made of the station at Tan-y-Bwlch for publicity purposes and stationmistress Bessie Jones spent much time in Welsh national costume, to the delight of both passengers and photographers. As well as posing for photographs, she would also take orders for refreshments and sell postcards of herself. In an undated view, she again poses, but here during a quiet moment. Her delightful stone cottage, built around 1897, stands where The Barn stood previously and it was from here that refreshments were dispensed. Note the verdant growth around the site which in earlier views of this place was somewhat lacking; also note the station nameboard, not usually seen in similar views. *Peter Johnson collection.*

More views of Bessie. *(above, left)* **With her cottage behind here, she poses as exchanging the token with the driver of TALIESIN.** *M.J.S. collection.* *(opposite, lower)* **Quite what this shot was meant to depict is unsure, as Bessie holds the train token in her left hand, whilst she appears to be handing a ticket to the passenger. Whatever, the rest of the travellers seem to find it all highly amusing! Meanwhile, with a healthy supply of coal atop the bunker, double-Fairlie TALIESIN has its water tanks replenished by fireman Tom Davies.** *Peter Johnson collection.* *(above, right)* **Here, in July 1936, Bessie plays temporary nursemaid to a very unsure-looking boy, believed to be her son Islwyn. In her right hand she holds more of those postcards. To the right, a mixed 'up' train can just be glimpsed.** *Harry Adams, Gerald Adams collection.*

(right) **A final look at pre-war Tan-y-Bwlch. In the late-1930s, double-Fairlie TALIESIN, renamed from LIVINGSTON THOMPSON in 1931, pauses on a down train. This was a period when poor performance was frequent and the presence of a second brake van, next to last vehicle in view, after two small Birminghams, suggests that this might have been an occasion when two trains were combined in an attempt to restore some order to the timetable. The coaches are in the many-hued 'rainbow train' liveries that the FR adopted during its association with the Welsh Highland Railway, in an attempt to drum up custom. The spur in the foreground ran to the goods shed and sidings. The weight on the furthest point lever indicates which way the road is set.** *M.J.S. collection.*

Prior to the introduction of steam to the FR in 1863, all services were horse-drawn. Passenger services were officially launched on 5th January 1865 and Penrhyn, serving the hamlet of Penrhyndeudraeth, was among the first stations opened. In 1887 the small but eminently serviceable station building, which had formerly served at Harbour station, Portmadoc until 1879, stands ready for its next quota of business. Note another double-armed signal post, standing by the short spur siding containing a wagon and the closeness of the line to the retaining wall, right. The enamel signs proclaim an unidentified 'best London paper' giving 'latest news', and Sunlight Soap, whilst the gas lamp seems rather large in relation to the size of the station building. On two occasions in later years, a second track was briefly added closer to the station. Preservation days have seen a genuine and largely successful attempt at recreating this scene, apart from the short siding, but the railway has hit objections to the resurrection of the signal post. *R.H.Bleasdale, FR Archives.*

That gas lamp is glimpsed again, in a view from July 1936 looking back up the line. Smoke from the unseen locomotive, a double-Fairlie, appears above the bogie brakevan, whilst the rear of the train is made up of empty slate wagons being returned to the quarries. *Hugh Tours, Martin Cook collection.*

Also in July 1936, PALMERSTON stands on the junction of the short siding while undertaking a brief spell of shunting. This siding was largely used to serve the local bakery and 1880s-vintage goods van No.129 may well have contained flour. *Hugh Tours, Martin Cook collection.*

(right) **Minffordd around 1897. Yet another posed shot, so beloved of Victorians, as the crew temporarily abandon their journey for their portrait by the single-Fairlie TALIESIN. Two four-wheeled Brown, Marshalls coaches lead the rake of two 1879-built Gloster Wagon Co. coaches in original condition and a bogie brakevan. Minffordd, built in 1872, was the first non-timber intermediate station. The fine 1887-vintage stone and slate building is glimpsed here, whilst to the right, another double-arm signal stands guard over a much more diminutive waiting shelter on the down 'platform'.** *FR Heritage collection.*

(below) **A decade earlier and this delightful posed photograph shows off the station to good advantage. JAMES SPOONER, the second double-Fairlie, delivered in 1872, heads a standard passenger train formation of two four-wheelers, two bogie coaches and a bogie van, as the train and station staff stand very proudly in their company uniforms.** *R.H.Bleasdale, FR Archives.*

(right) **A rare view of the diminutive 'down' waiting shelter. Although seen in 1955, when the ravages of time were most definitely having their effect, it can be seen that the facilities on this side of the line would never have been that opulent! The apparently newer part of the front wall, was merely a board covering rotten timber! Time had played its part by 5th May 1956, however, when PRINCE and a chain had little problem in effecting demolition!** *Robin Butterell*

In slightly happier times, on 8th July 1936, that shelter is again seen, to the left of double-Fairlie TALIESIN as it waits to continue on the last leg of the journey to Portmadoc. Typical Thirties fashions predominate among the onlookers in the obviously pleasant late afternoon summer sunshine. Since Bleasdale's day, above, the main station chimneys have been reduced in height, but there has been the addition of telegraph wires and receiving pots. Note the directions to the GWR station and its approach ramp, right. *S.W.Baker, FR Heritage collection.*

By Monday, 14th July 1947, roughly the same view looks altogether different. Gone is the clean and prosperous air, with nature once more regaining a hold. But it is not dead, it merely sleepeth! *Robin Butterell.*

The main workshops for the railway were situated at Boston Lodge, virtually at the end of the continuous falling gradient. Immediately past the Halt, opened in the late-1920s, and just before the line reached the Works site from the north, it passed the original engine shed. Seen on 4th August 1925, it is in 'final' condition, the state it was in when in constant use. The right hand, two-road shed was built in 1863, to house the then new England locomotives, with the corrugated iron addition coming some twenty years later, to accommodate MERDDIN EMRYS and LIVINGSTON THOMPSON. Fittingly, when viewed on this day, the incumbents were two England 0-4-0s, PRINCE, left and WELSH PONY. The 'main line' can be seen squeezing between shed and boundary wall, with a water tower extreme right. Note also the post of 'down' distant for Boston Lodge signal box. *H.G.W. Household, Peter Johnson collection.*

Seen nearly forty years prior to the viewabove, in 1887, the shed yard is a hive of activity, with three locomotives posed for the photgrapher. From l to r, MERDDIN EMRYS, the rear of single-Fairlie TALLIESIN, and PRINCESS are seen, with locomotive superintendent William Williams overseeing matters. The corrugated-iron extension to the shed, on the left, is barely a year old, having been built to accomodate the two new double-Fairlies, MERDDIN EMRYS and LIVINGSTON THOMPSON. Note that this and the main shed are fitted with very tall smoke vents. These were vunerable to wind and weather - their reducing numbers are useful for dating photographs of the shed. *R.H.Bleasdale, Roger Griffiths collection.*

(top) The transition, quite swift and dramatic in hindsight, from the diminutive 0-4-0 England tanks of 1863 to the double-Fairlies - the first, LITTLE WONDER, was delivered just six years later, in the summer of 1869 - as has been well documented elsewhere and their success and importance is beyond question. By the mid-1870s, however, there was perceived to be a need for something in between. The result - TALIESIN, an 0-4-4T single-Fairlie, delivered from Vulcan Foundry in 1876. Effectively half a 'double', this was the first locomotive on the railway to be blessed with the name and is not to be confused with the re-naming of LIVINGSTON THOMPSON at a later date. Seen in the yard of Boston Lodge Works a decade or so after delivery, the cab has been adjusted - there were problems with clearances virtually on arrival at the FR! - the early lined livery with fleur-de-lys over the nameplate has disappeared, a handrail and greater capacity FR sandpots have been fitted to and by the smokebox, as well as a toolbox atop the tank. A little over 110 years later, a recreation of this locomotive entered traffic on the restored FR on 1st May 1999. *R .H. Bleasdale, FR Archives.*

The original TALIESIN, above, effectively ceased to function around 1927, when a new boiler was required but not sanctioned. Withdrawn from stock in 1931, the name was transferred to the existing double-Fairlie LIVINGSTON THOMPSON (to further confuse matters, this engine was renamed EARL OF MERIONETH in 1961!). In August 1936, the new incarnation is seen at Portmadoc Harbour station (centre), having brought its train from Blaenau Ffestiniog. The fireman poses for his picture before taking the locomotive to the water tower and then running round his train. Behind is ex-curly-roofed bogie brakevan No.2, now rebodied. Happily, this carriage survives to the present day as No.10. *John F.Clay.* The first steam locomotive supplied to the FR in 1863 was PRINCESS. Originally named THE PRINCESS and imaginatively numbered No. 1(!), the locomotive is seen in original condition (bottom) in 1871, complete with the first design of sanders that proved inadequate, standing alongside the original Harbour station buildings. The decidedly primitive Brown, Marshalls open carriage, built without roof and merely covered in a tarpaulin arrangement, stands next to THE PRINCESS and offers little extra protection from the elements to that given to the locomotive crew! PRINCESS was rebuilt to full saddle-tank design in 1891. *FR Co.,MJS collection.*

Into the 1890s (post-1896), double-Fairlies have arrived and Harbour station has seen much development. LIVINGSTON THOMPSON appears to be ready to haul a 'start of the week' formation train, with a short 'quarrymen's train', comprising two quarrymen's and two Ashbury four-wheel Parliamentary coaches, at the head of a standard passenger rake. Note the myriad of tall ship masts in the wharf beyond. *Peter Treloar collection.*

Back to 1936 and the two remaining double-Fairlies, TALIESIN and MERDDIN EMRYS unusually stand side-by-side in Harbour station on a grey July day. The carriage sidings look ready to serve a great number of travellers, but at that period it is unlikely that much of it would have been needed in the short term. Note the lower-quadrant starter signal by the goods shed and the LM&SR notice board on the station wall. *Hugh Tours, Martin Cook collection.*

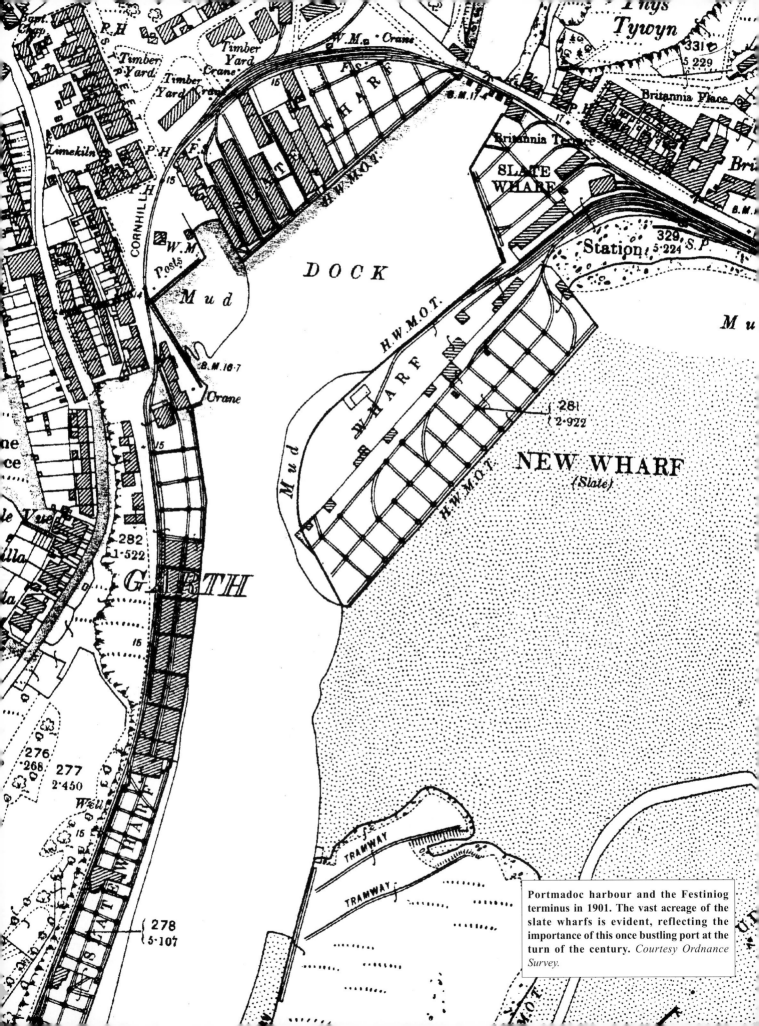

Portmadoc harbour and the Festiniog terminus in 1901. The vast acreage of the slate wharfs is evident, reflecting the importance of this once bustling port at the turn of the century. *Courtesy Ordnance Survey.*

Finally, we have reached the destination of our 'slate run' down from Blaenau Ffestiniog. We look at the main area of FR operations as seen from across the harbour, giving an idea of the setting for the 'headquarters' of the railway and its most opportune siting. Viewed from half-way up the hill towards Borth-y-Gest, prodigious quantities of slate stand awaiting shipment, covering virtually every available inch of space. The Cob can be seen running in from the right hand side, bringing the railway past Britannia Foundry and into Harbour station, with tracks then continuing towards the camera, onto South Snowdon wharf. Quite possibly the scene on a Sunday, seven tall masted ships can be seen, all resting at anchor despite the obvious high tide, together with one of the Portmadoc Harbour Commissioners' steam paddle tugs, *SNOWDONIA* or *WAVE OF LIFE*. These latter were used to haul four or five sailing vessels at a time out into the open water of Traeth Mawr, for them to begin their voyages. In the boatyard, two more schooners are under construction. Undated, the view is believed to be around the turn of the century, but is definitely post-1887, the year R.H.Bleasdale visited to photograph the railway and had painted white a section of the Cob fencing, as a backdrop to posed locomotives. This can be seen to the right of the station area, which contains a quarrymen's train rake and a passenger set on the sidings. At this time, the FR was earning healthy amounts from all this activity, which took slate to many parts of the world. *Peter Johnson collection.*

5th October 1951. **As we finished the last chapter with a general view of Harbour station and its environs, so we begin there again, this time in the 'interregnum' years between closure and re-opening and looking at the view from the Cob and Traeth Mawr embankment, with Moel-y-Gest rising majestically in the background. The ex-slate wharf now stands empty and the houses rising above the area look down on inactivity. The old FR 'calling-on' signal gantry, erected in 1929 and originally used at Duffws, still stands, guarding the entrance to the station, but with only the one arm remaining, indicating that in the run-down of traffic prior to final closure only the station tracks were used. In happier times, the left-hand arm controlled access to South Snowdon wharf and the carriage sidings, whilst that on the right signalled for the goods shed (seen straight ahead) and across Britannia bridge.** *Hugh Ballantyne.*

5th October 1951. **A leisurely walk in the pleasant autumn afternoon sunshine brings us to a remarkable sight. A yard full of empty slate wagons and other stock stands just as left five years earlier, when the railway was abruptly abandoned. Although Robert Evans, General Manager and the last employee of the company at the time of closure, kept an eye on things here and at Boston Lodge, it is a sign of the times that nothing has apparently been touched, with all the station windows intact and no signs of vandalism. Whilst potentially a source of stock and spares, some of the wagons were not serviceable and the whole view gives some idea of the task facing the would-be preservationists at this time, especially at a time when the country was still finding its feet after the effects of world war and railway preservation was certainly not the accepted norm that it is today.** *Hugh Ballantyne.*

Chapter Two:
1951 - 1960.

As seen at the close of the last chapter, the Festiniog Railway lay moribund after closure in 1946. In 1950, the Company held an Extraordinary General Meeting, where it was agreed that permission for abandonment should be sought from the Minister of Transport. Not having the relevant authority, the Minister refused permission in October of that year. As we have seen, an Act of Parliament was required and without the necessary wherewithal to achieve this, the position became somewhat stagnated. This might have been the status quo for many years, had it not been for the vision and imagination of a few far-sighted individuals.

The series of events and the relationship between the various individuals that came to eventually formulate the rescue plan are both complex and convoluted, and finding one's way through them is about as easy as breaching a barbed-wire fence! Suffice to say that many who took the reins and steered matters to the successful purchase of the railway in 1954, were either around or in the background at the dawning of 1951, the start of our period of interest here.

Many grand schemes and great achievements come about by happy coincidence and the saving of the FR is no exception. Allan Garraway, who later became the railway's first full-time manager and engineer - and General Manager from 1958 - had joined the nascent Talyllyn Railway Preservation Society in 1950. A meeting with Bill Harvey (BR shedmaster at Norwich) led to them both visiting the TR in July 1951, to act as volunteers. They visited the Festiniog whilst in North Wales and both were hooked, impressed by the scale and standard of engineering on the line.

A letter to the railway press by teenager Leonard Heath-Humphrys led to a meeting in Bristol on 8th September 1951, at which Allan met others who were of a like mind and who would become 'household' names on the railway in succeeding years. Prior to this, J.I.C.Boyd, who had and still retains a deep interest in things narrow gauge, had attended a meeting in Portmadoc on 20th April 1951, where it was found that the remaining slate quarries and local authorities were in favour of restoration. On numerous occasions he was party to correspondence and negotiations with the old FR Co., but to no avail. In September, with official local support dissipating, he gave up on the idea and returned his enthusiasm to the Talyllyn. However, his contact with Lord Northesk led to the latter relating the plight of the FR to one Alan Pegler, who was to become important in our story in the following year.

Meetings and negotiations with the old FR Co. continued in 1952, with members of that Bristol meeting driving matters forward. At this stage, some of those previously in the background came into the frame, not least through their involvement with a Doncaster Works centenary special train; and during the year the Festiniog Railway Preservation Society was proposed. January 1953 saw a meeting of the Society at the Great Northern Hotel in King's Cross, London with Alan Pegler and others so far 'in the background' in attendance. Mr Pegler Snr. was a man of means and his son approached him regarding the possibility of having some funds for the rescue of the FR. Initial reaction was not favourable (!), but towards the end of 1953 he relented, on the proviso that Alan Pegler had some control over affairs. FRPS committee meetings were held into 1954, followed by further discussions and negotiations which finally led to a cheque for £2,000 being handed over and Alan Pegler and his nominees taking control of the FR from 24th June 1954.

Meanwhile during 1954, visits on the ground had investigated what should or, more importantly, what *could* be saved. Allan Garraway, Bill Harvey and Morris Jones moved the first train for eight years - digging through the accumulated sand blown into Boston Lodge Works yard - managing to haul two coaches across the Cob to Harbour station. The 6th November saw a special run to Minffordd, for directors and guests, comprising ex-World War 1 Simplex and coach No.11. On 24th December, the Festiniog Railway Society Ltd. was incorporated and the stage was set for progress. On a sad note, with hindsight, the remains of ex-Welsh Highland MOEL TRYFAN were sold for scrap, along with much else that was not identified for further use, as funds were desperately needed for the restoration of PRINCE and to purchase new sleepers.

Into 1955 and two events gave conflicting signals of hope and threat. On 5th March, a group of the volunteers managed to overcome years of neglect, verdant growth and a very damp

11th October 1951. **Six days later and, further up the line, there is yet more sign of abandonment and gentle dereliction. The open space that was Tan-y-Bwlch station lies windswept and apparently unloved, although not strictly true, as Bessie Jones and husband Will still lived in the station house and Will regularly lubricated the points. The goods shed door, however, has certainly seen better days and the wooden crane close by looks near to a state of collapse. This makes for a fascinating comparison with the same vantage point at the end of the Millennium, after the attentions of the restorers.** *Hugh Ballantyne.*

12th October 1951. One day on and yet further up the line, Tanygrisiau station and surroundings stand like some Wild West ghost town. On can almost anticipate the tumbleweed blowing down the tracks! A wagon has moved from the small turntable since the view seen in the last chapter, but otherwise the scene is as it had remained for years, a veritable _Marie Celeste_ of the railway world. _Hugh Ballantyne._

Moelwyn tunnel to reach the old 'joint' FR/GWR station in Blaenau, using the Simplex with coach No.17 and van No.1; but at the same time, a Bill was being proposed to Parliament, for a hydro-electric power station at Tanygrisiau that would obliterate some of the very route that these intrepid explorers had just conquered! It was hoped that substantial compensation would flow from this, but it was not to• be. Additionally, residents of Tanygrisiau and Blaenau Ffestiniog were in favour of the hydro-electric scheme and the jobs it was hoped it would bring, and were not in favour of the FR, which was perceived to be 'queering the pitch'. However, 1955 did see the railway re-open to the public.

Up to this point, the only form of traction that was operative was the petrol-driven Simplex tractor. This opened the season on 23rd July, hauling two coaches across the Cob to Boston Lodge Halt, advertised as 'for Port Meirion'. Trains ran on the half-hour from Portmadoc between 10.30 a.m. and 5.30 p.m., excepting 12.30, and returned on the following hour. If the volunteers had had doubts as to the viability of their dreams, they need not have worried as the public duly supported this service, albeit of very short length.

Meanwhile, in Boston Lodge Works, efforts to restore PRINCE to 'working order' were reaching conclusion. The locomotive re-entered service on 3rd August, having steamed across the Cob for the first time the previous evening - nine years to the day since PRINCESS had last run. From there not having been a public train service for nine years, the

railway now had two locomotives at its disposal. Elsewhere, the need for 'new' rails, and there being no foreseeable possibility of trains returning there, saw the flat bottomed track on the Dinas branch lifted in November and sold to raise funds.

As has been the case ever since, the FR was not about to rest on its laurels. In 1954, the Central Electricity Authority (predecessor of the Central Electricty Generating Board) had toured and inspected the line, in an effort to show that the railway was not capable of re-opening. The gallant volunteers, however - and now with Allan Garraway in his full-time capacity - were not about to take this lying down. They re-doubled their efforts to show that this was not the case, and that they could make real, noticeable progress.

Passenger services were extended to Minffordd on 19th May 1956 - now on the hour between 11 a.m. and 5 p.m. from Portmadoc and returning on the half-hour - a new water tank having been installed at Harbour station to service locomotives. The Baldwin tractor, now diesel-powered and later to be named MOELWYN, and double-Fairlie TALIESIN joined the locomotive roster, the latter on 4th September, although not on regular duties until the following year. Pen Cob Halt, by Boston Lodge Works, was added as a 'request' stop. Looking in the opposite direction from Harbour station to the way that the FR was being reborn, it had been realised in 1953 that it was not feasible to restore traffic to the old Welsh Highland Railway and, therefore, the tracks along High

14th October 1951. **Like Harbour station, Boston Lodge was littered at this time with abandoned stock. On this date, there stands, from left to right, a corner of coach No.15, bogie coach No.19, wagon No.1017, the remains of ex-WHR single-Fairlie MOEL TRYFAN, almost unrecognisable amongst the bushes!, and a corner of No.16. Again, the glass in the windows is largely intact and, apart from the odd slate missing on the roof, the Works look as though their doors merely stand closed awaiting re-opening. Originally built in connection with the 1807 Act of Parliament, authorising construction of the Cob, and so titled in recognition that William Madocks was MP for Boston, Lincs. and still in full use nearly two hundred years later, Boston Lodge is the oldest continuously occupied railway Works in the world.** *Hugh Ballantyne.*

August 1952. **The view above was repeated many times during the period of closure, but few visitors ventured as far as climbing the hill behind the Works, to capture this angle. Left foreground is the roof of the joiner's shop and beyond that the smithy, with PALMERSTON outside. The building in front of the locomotive was the foundry, with the chimney of the boiler house - so long a landmark - in front of the machine shop and pattern loft. To the right of the chimney and parallel to the above buildings, were the sawmill (with odd-looking exhaust), the brass foundry (with roof ventilator and chimney behind) and a line of old slate wagons. At right-angles to this, was the old oil store - now S&T - and the long roof, upper right, belonged to Nos.1 and 2 Boston Lodge - staff cottages. By the time of preservation, the sawmill roof had collapsed and the building was soon demolished.** *J.B.Snell.*

Street, west of Britannia Bridge, were lifted in November 1956.

1957 saw further progress and extension, with Penrhyn station re-opening from 20th April and a peak-season evening train added to the timetable. A loop line was specially installed at this temporary terminus, to enable engines to run-round. On the stock front, coaches 11 and 12 (ex- bogie brake vans 4 and 5 of 1880), 17 (a Spooner bogie composite coach of 1876) and Ashbury No.23 of 1894, had settled into regular work on passenger trains, with No.12 having been converted in 1956 to serve as a buffet car.

During the year attention was also turned to the trackbed further north, with locomotives often used in pulling trees bodily away from track or lineside! Progress north of Moelwyn tunnel was curtailed during the year, when rails were lifted as far as the northern portal, in connection with the power station scheme.

For 1958, the timetable showed connections with the BR Western Region stations at Portmadoc and Minffordd and, for the first time, looked towards the future, by stating 'service temporarily suspended' for Dduallt, Tan-y-grisiau *(sic)* and Blaenau Ffestiniog. It would be twenty-four years before the latter was finally reached! What the timetable also reflected was the opening to Tan-y-Bwlch from 5th April - thanks in no small part to Keith Catchpole and his band of enthusiastic and hard-working schoolboys from Enfield in August/ September 1957 - with the longer journey time (now 45 minutes, as opposed to 20 minutes to Penrhyn during the 1957 season) leading to a reduction in the number of trains - down to three plus the evening run in peak-season.

What was also happening, was that the railway was being almost overwhelmed by its own success. With many trains being literally full to overflowing, despite most of them being made up of six bogie coaches, three ancient four-wheelers were hastily made ready, to form a relief train, called the 'Flea',

hauled by PRINCE. These four-wheelers later became affectionately known as 'Bug Boxes'! Under normal circumstances, all other trains were operated by TALIESIN. On a more domestic note, the old water tank at Tan-y-Bwlch had passed its 'use-by' date and was scrapped, being replaced in January by a newer, though second-hand, example from Laxfield, Suffolk.

Outside influences have constantly affected the FR and during those early restoration years, there were occasionally distractions that it could have done without; the operating staff could so easily have taken their 'eyes off the ball'. In 1959, in connection with the construction of Trawsfynydd Nuclear Power Station, the South Snowdon wharf, by Harbour station, was identified as a site for unloading heavy electrical equipment, before being shipped by road to its destination. In connection with these plans, the road access around Harbour station building was to be widened and, to accommodate this, the gentlemen's toilet at the southern end of the platform was demolished. As it happened, another wharf was then preferred and this small building disappeared unnecessarily.

A more positive development in 1959 was the first steaming of MERDDIN EMRYS. The boiler, having been overhauled by Vulcan Foundry, was given a successful steam test in August. The double boiler, smokeboxes and bogies, denuded of cab, tanks and other fittings looked most unusual. It was, however, to be two more years before the locomotive re-entered traffic.

Into the next decade and it was largely a matter of consolidation before further pushes north could be achieved. The Trawsfynydd project brought disruption, with the rebuilding of Rhiw Plas bridge, between Boston Lodge and Minffordd, necessitating a temporary diversion of the road across the railway by level crossing, whilst the bridge was rebuilt. Spoil from the site was taken north to Tan-y-Bwlch by TALIESIN, and used to fill a hole there by the road bridge. The operating department could not let this hamper services too much, however, as the railway needed all the revenue it could muster. Although still running healthily full trains, there were no outside benefactors queuing up to inject funds into the railway and running an historic - and largely worn out - venture took every penny that could be found. Happily, it was reported that Easter 1960 passenger numbers showed a 30% increase over the previous Easter!

At Harbour station, permission had been granted to turn the 'townside' wharf area into a car park and this was achieved in 1960, allowing intending travellers to enter the station from this point, rather than along the platform as previously. On 13th July, BBC Television did a 'live' broadcast from the railway and the effect of this was dramatic, the year's traffic ending 33% up on 1959 and breaking all records. To accommodate traffic, coach No.15 (a Brown, Marshalls composite bogie of 1871) was hastily made serviceable in August, but entered traffic unfinished and in primer, going back each night to Boston Lodge for more work to be undertaken!

By the end of the year, 100,000 journeys had been recorded for the first time and things were looking up. Traffic was taking its toll on the track, however, and the 1960/61 winter season was set for much permanent way work to be done, to be ready for the next year's season.

27th October 1954. In late 1954, a survey of the whole line was undertaken by the, then, British Electricity Authority, to assess the feasibility of re-opening the railway, as proposed by the preservationists and to judge the effects on them of the planned new reservoir near Tanygrisiau. A series of photographs was taken, showing the condition of the route. This shows the appearance (or otherwise!) of the track immediately north of Penrhyn station, with the level crossing gates firmly shut against the railway. The white house in the distance now plays host to many visitors to the railway each year, but this view is now shielded by tree growth. *Central Electric Authority, FR Archives.*

27 October 1954. As seen in the first chapter, the trackbed between Moelwyn tunnel and Tanygrisiau was flooded in connection with the new power station scheme. The station and village of Tanygrisiau lie in the mist to the right of the rocky outcrop in the mid-distance; everything between them and the photographer was swallowed up by the Llyn Ystradau floodwater, including the dwelling to the left and this gives some indication of the huge volume of water created by the scheme. The railway can be seen running from the tunnel, to the right and heading north around the base of the outcrop, whilst the sheep lazily graze, blissfully unaware of the change about to hit their pasture. *Central Electric Authority, FR Archives*

(left) 27 October 1954. This view was captioned, "Condition of railway track south-west of Foundry House, Tanygrisiau". The state of the bull-head rails appears reasonable, but the sleepers certainly have seen better days! The rebuilding of the railway, occasioned by the creation of the reservoir, meant that the tracks reached the station area along a higher approach than seen here. The hydro-electric scheme cleared the area of rails and this vantage point is now part of the roadway leading to the station's car park, the visitor centre and ultimately, following the curvature round to the left, the power station itself. The reservoir waters now lap at this retaining wall, submerging the barn and enclosure walls seen here. *Central Electric Authority, FR Archives*

(below) March 1955. A last look at the old FR alignment in Blaenau Ffestiniog, showing the shared Central station, with the ex-GWR standard gauge tracks to the left. At this time, the route from Porthmadog was still extant and there were thoughts of eventual restoration to this point. This straightforward plan was scotched, however, by the 1962/3 severing of the trackbed at Stesion Fain, in connection with the new road from the town to Tanygrisiau. All was not lost, however, as both narrow and standard gauge rails restored a link to this part of the town in 1982, but with their respective routes reversed, relative to the view here. The path of the pre-1932 'up' line to Duffws can be seen to the right of the track still in use at this time by Oakeley Quarry slate trains. *G.E.Baddeley, Peter Johnson collection.*

(right) Easter 1955. The years 1954/5 saw much preliminary work by the volunteers, rescuing the trackbed from the attentions of nature among other things, in preparation for opening services to the public. Here, at Minffordd station, much earnest discussion is taking place, perhaps considering what should be done next, but certainly relieved and celebrating the first access of a train of any sort into the loop for nine years. The very first preservationist train had reached Minffordd on the previous 6th November. Some indication of the amount of work needed just to make the rails visible again, can be judged from comparison of old 'up' (right) and 'down' lines (left). Slate wagons stand on the 'up' tracks, whilst the motive power in the loop is provided by the Simplex tractor. David Rouse, seen in the Frontispiece photograph, is again seen here, on the locomotive in oilskins, whilst John Halsall, later working in the carriage works, stands half-facing the camera, in battledress blouse, hands on hips. *J.B.Snell*.

(middle) At this time, Minffordd station building was also receiving attention. Twenty-six years since passengers joined or left a train here, the years have obviously not been kind. Slates stand infront of the old waiting room, having been removed from the roof timbers. These are in the process of being renovated, with the ladder giving access and waiting for the photographer to put down his camera and restart work! The delightful lantern that rested at the base of the curved iron support is missing, its base covered by a sack. *Robin Butterell*.

At the same time as above, a motley-looking octet take a break from their labours. Left to right, are: Max Sinclair, Brian Rogers, Alan Pratt, ?, Robin Butterell, Graham Vincent, Peter Hollins and Tony White. *Robin Butterell collection.*

29th May 1955. **Oh those innocent days before the Health & Safety Executive came to rule our lives! A group of excited supporters/ enthusiasts/volunteers stand at Harbour station, before preparing to make an exploratory trip as far up the line as they can reach. The Simplex is again the motive power - virtually the only thing that would run successfully at this time - though with the front now in skeletal form, showing the very bare bones! Crack BR engine driver Bill Hoole walks towards the camera, about to take charge of the tractor, whilst Geoff Stones, in white shirt and the rest will ride in bogie brakevan No.10 behind.** *Hugh Ballantyne.*

29th May 1955. **Later that day and whoops! - the end of this particular journey. The ducket of No.10 had a habit of hitting the stone walls, but here, perhaps not totally surprisingly, given the inherited state of the track, the tractor has come to grief, having derailed, half a mile or so short of Tan-y-Bwlch. A concentrated knot of onlookers and advisers gather round, assessing the situation, but judging from the smiles on the faces of those by the locomotive and the casual stance of the young ladies by the carriage, things are presumably not too serious.** *Hugh Ballantyne.*

31st May 1955. **A view that seems to confirm a more casual era and the sometimes ad-hoc, 'Heath Robinson-ish' methods of working. Raised on a single jack and balanced on sleepers, the bogie of brakevan No.12 is wheeled out for attention. Bill Hoole, left, is again on hand to share his experience. With a sister coach, (No.11, ex-No.4) No.12 (ex-No.5) was built in 1880, with traditional roofline and measuring nearly 4 ft. longer than the earlier three. Initially built purely as brakevans, they were rebuilt for passenger use at Boston Lodge around 1930, with No.12 serving as a buffet car on the restored FR. The motive power, standing in front of the Cleminson six-wheeler, is BUSTA, a petrol-driven 2-2-0, reportedly an ex-WHR permanent way trolley.** *Hugh Ballantyne.*

(right) 4th August 1955. Remains of a toastrack! In 1923 the FR bought six open-sided bogie coaches of War Department design from Robert Hudson Ltd. Numbered between 37 and 42, they had room for 32 passengers and cost just £155 each, but were not a success. Less than a decade later, all had been withdrawn from passenger use, although two were temporarily restored in the last period of the railway's normal operations. Nicknamed 'toastracks' due to their design, an unidentified member of the type lies abandoned outside the deteriorating remains of the original engine shed at Boston Lodge. *John S.Macfarlane.*

(bottom) 4th August 1955. After a great deal of 'blood, sweat and tears', the railway re-opened to passenger traffic in 1955, with the first train running on 23rd July, hauled by the Simplex. Initially, trains ran to Boston Lodge Halt, with a laborious arrangement for return traffic, as there was no run-round facility at the Halt. PRINCE was the first steam locomotive to be restored. Fitted with a new boiler that had been ordered during the War, he entered service once more on 5th August 1955. This view, then, is the last day of the Simplex having the railway to itself. It stands in Harbour station, waiting to be the 10.30 a.m. departure, with a nearly full ex-WHR/NWNGR coach No.23. The many young children visible in the coach indicate that families are already being attracted to the railway, rather than just enthusiasts and it is this market that has helped the railway to grow and develop. *John S.Macfarlane.*

(opposite, top) 15th March 1956. Overcoming perilous track conditions, the intrepid volunteers managed to finally traverse the whole length of the FR to the site of the old Stesion Fain on 5th March 1955. Along the way, they cleared the pathway as necessary and retrieved items felt to be of use. One such visit is seen here early the following year by the station water tower, with a train comprising old slate wagons. At this time, the old LNWR/LMS station was being rebuilt by British Railways, it having burnt down in 1951. The new retaining wall and rising brick columns of the station building itself, can be seen to the left, with workmen busy on their scaffolding. In the background, the footbridge over the original route of the FR can be seen above and beyond the two volunteers. *Geoff Charles, Peter Johnson collection.*

(right) 21st June 1956. You win some, you lose some! To the left, the BR station now has roof structures in place, but across the road, the old FR station is being dismantled. The work being undertaken by contractors, the sale of the canopy raised valuable funds for the nascent railway. That footbridge and the original FR entrance to Blaenau Ffestiniog can still be seen past the station canopy, which has already lost its roof and bargeboards. Window frames have also been removed from the old refreshment room and bricks will soon follow, to provide hardcore. *Brian Hilton, Peter Treloar collection.*

9th August 1956. Celebrating a year of renewed service, PRINCE slows to bring its three-coach train to a halt at Pen Cob Halt. The 'station' sign exhorts 'Passengers requiring to board the train, please signal the driver'. Opened in May 1956, the site of this halt was far from satisfactory and as the railway progressed northwards, it ceased to be a stopping place from 5th November 1957. *R.K.Blencowe, Peter Treloar collection.*

(opposite, bottom) April 1956. MERDDIN EMRYS was the last double-Fairlie in use prior to the line's closure in 1946. Like so much of the rest of the railway, the locomotive was merely dumped after its last shift, with water still in the boiler and tanks and coal still in the bunkers. This led to greater deterioration in condition than would otherwise have been the case and meant that the preservationists had a harder job to restore it to working condition. Completion was eventually achieved, however, by 1961. For the railway's AGM in March 1956, the locomotive was posed, unrestored, in Harbour station, along with coaches 15, 17, 22, 23 and 12. This unusual view from the signal post by the goods shed, right, shows that posed train, with locomotive definitely in need of attention! The wharf siding is still visible, swinging to the left just past the gentleman in the long black coat. MERDDIN EMRYS was returned to Boston Lodge on 29th April. *J.B.Snell.*

23rd April 1957. **On this day, members of the Imperial College Railway Society took a train comprising diesel MOELWYN and a handful of wagons as far as Moelwyn tunnel, inspecting the route and recovering whatever might be useful to the railway, this time from the northern end of the tunnel, before tracks were finally lifted there. The first view is at Tyler's Curve, south of Tan-y-Bwlch, where time is taken to admire the view across the Vale of Ffestiniog. It is obvious that a certain amount of clearance is needed before services can be restored here!**

Lunch at Dduallt. Ever an isolated spot, it could be described as peaceful or desolate, depending on the season, weather or personal inclination. On this fine spring day, the former description would be appropriate. The station re-opened to passengers from 6th April 1968.

Having run round its train at Dduallt, MOELWYN has pushed its load up to the tunnel's southern entrance, from where some of the more intrepid visitors have inspected the conditions inside. Judging by the bare feet of the young man coming towards us, the winter rains have found their way to the tunnel floor! This is a fine portrait of MOELWYN and its train, which appears to now contain all manner of wood and metalwork. Built in America for World War 1 use in France, the engine was purchased by the FR in 1925 and even saw very brief duties on the WHR. Newly-fitted in August 1956 with a Gardner 3LW diesel engine, it is here still running as an 0-4-0. Later in 1957 a ponytruck was fitted to improve the ride and the tractor was named MOELWYN, (a 'Welsh' pun on the name of its makers - Baldwin!). *all B.P.Pask.*

June 1957. As mentioned in the previous chapter, Penrhyn station was renovated by the volunteers in readiness for the re-opening to this point on 30th March 1957. Becoming the temporary northern terminus, while work continued on the stretch to Tan-y-Bwlch, a loop line was installed closer to the station building, to facilitate the running round of locomotives. From this elevated vantage point, some of the success with the building can be seen, as can the open valley beyond. For many years into this century, the village of Penrhyn was without direct access to the valley road and the place saw little change. This altered with the construction of the A4085's direct route and this view across the valley is now dramatically altered. This being late afternoon, one presumes that this is PRINCE's last run down for the day; there is precious little evidence of a sufficient supply of coal! *Peter Treloar.*

June 1957. Slightly earlier in the day, PRINCE coasts down the falling gradient from Penrhyn. *Peter Treloar.*

27th June 1957. **Taking the opportunity of a break in train movements, Will Jones, a lengthman for the FR from 1922, and assistant (Evie Lloyd?) get to grips with some infrastructure work. In the early days of preservation, track gave as much cause for concern as the locomotives - if not more! - and every possible opportunity was taken for repairs. Without funds for wholesale replacement, spot re-sleepering, to eliminate the worst problems, was the order of the day, as seen here just above Minffordd. There were few trains each day and the trolley on which sleepers had been brought up, could be run back to the station in time to clear the line. Ballast has been cleared and it is obviously warm work, with coats abandoned on the wall.** *Peter Treloar.*

2nd September 1957. During 1957, teacher - and FR driver - Keith Catchpole brought parties of his Enfield schoolboys to work on the railway. In groups of fifty, they would travel by 56-seater coach, bringing 'everything' with them, including tools and food and staying with 20+ families in the area. During the long summer break of 1957, they spent a fortnight fighting their way forward from Penrhyn towards Tan-y-Bwlch. The way was extremely arduous, with trees and bushes overgrowing the line to form a tunnel at some points (!), and the track sat precariously in places, unattended for eleven years. The Baldwin being unavailable, PRINCE was commandeered for the boys' train, comprising brakevan No.10. This latter had windows removed because of the 'whipping' action of the lineside tree branches! PRINCE had only limited water capacity and the exertions meant rapid use of this. The solution was for the locomotive to travel back to Penrhyn at lunch times, to join the service train hauled by TALIESIN, for the run back to Harbour station. As seen here, the train has arrived back in Porthmadog and TALIESIN is being uncoupled, to release PRINCE and to permit that engine to run to the water tower. It was through the boys' efforts during this summer session that the railway once again reached Tan-y-Bwlch and facilitated the re-opening to that station the following spring. Over a thirty year period, 1674 'Tadpoles', as Keith's boys became known, worked on the FR, one or two still being there in 1999. *B.P.Pask.*

2nd September 1957. The tide is out and the road alongside the Cob virtually empty, as PRINCE and TALIESIN make their way home to Boston Lodge, drivers Keith Catchpole and Allan Garraway at the controls, the relative day's efforts completed. At this time, the double-Fairlie would normally haul the day's trains, having been finally returned to steam exactly one year before this view, after the literal abandonment mid-repair in 1946. *B.P.Pask.*

8th September 1957. **A different view of the Cob, seen from high above Boston Lodge and looking towards Porthmadog. Moel-y-Gest dominates the skyline, whilst the marshland around the Afon Glaslyn, right, is flooded at high tide. At one mile in length, the massive achievement of William Madocks in building this structure, against many obstacles both natural and financial, can be judged from this angle.** *B.P.Pask.*

September 1957. **As is mentioned elsewhere, 1873-vintage bogie brakevan No.10 (originally No.2) was the only one of the original trio to survive into preservation. Rebuilt in 1921 at Boston Lodge, with a conventional roof line from the initial curly shape and at that time providing passenger accommodation, the van is seen at Harbour station, showing signs of use on early clearance trains. All the glass is missing from the windows, as is the guard's footboard, and the ducket is very battered.** *B.P.Pask.*

(opposite) 26th April 1958. **Tan-y-Bwlch station was re-opened to traffic on 5th April 1958, in time for Easter and the new season; the extension to the route, not surprisingly, generating much interest. Three weeks later the station is host to the longest train so far run under preservation, on the occasion of the FR Society AGM. Interested Society members, cameras much in evidence, inspect the train before the return trip. Driver and Manager Allan Garraway strides round his locomotive to join the fireman, both with daffodil buttonholes in honour of the occasion! Note the influx of period cars - a sign of things to come!** *B.P.Pask.*

(above) 22nd September 1957. No.10 is again seen, coupled to PRINCE on the locomotive's first visit to the south portal of Moelwyn tunnel since re-opening. Once again, the wider space encompassed by the wall can be seen, right, at this isolated spot, harking back to the pre-steam days when horses were changed here. *Allan Garraway, Peter Johnson collection.*

(right) Winter 1957. Now completely abandoned, the run into Blaenau Ffestiniog stands left to the elements. The late-19th century signal still stands with its arm, whilst under the bridge the railway's Glan-y-Pwll presence can be seen the other side of the closed level crossing gates. *Martin Cook collection.*

26th April 1958. **Seen moments before TALIESIN coupled-up, bogie brakevan No.11 stands at the bottom end of the train, fitted out as a first class observation car and smartly finished in green livery with red ends, complete with a stylised '1' and FR crest.** *B.P.Pask.*

26th April 1958. **Present on the same day, 'Small Birmingham' No.3 is pictured in the siding by the goods shed at Tan-y-Bwlch. Its condition is obviously too poor to be used in revenue trains, but it had given good service as a mess hut for the staff repairing track between Penrhyn and Tan-y-Bwlch during the winter prior to the opening.** *B.P.Pask.*

Summer 1958. **The tourist season is now in full swing and judging by the fashions, the weather is warmer. In a scene that would now give the H&SE a heart attack, passengers wander at will, coming to watch TALIESIN taking refreshment from the old water tank or merely stretching their legs; the young lad gazes longingly at the hidden world of the footplate! Note No.3 emblazoned on the buffer plate, and the high heels on uneven ground. Suits also predominate amongst the men - how fashions have changed!** *Peter Treloar.*

3rd September 1958. **In 1955, PRINCE had been restored to restart traffic as he had been found in the middle of a general overhaul and with a new boiler part-fitted. TALIESIN and MERDDIN EMRYS had followed, as they had again been mid-overhaul and required for increasing traffic respectively. 1863-vintage No.1 PRINCESS, the last locomotive in service under the old company, and No.5 WELSH PONY, from 1867, were hopefully to follow and here await their respective fates, stored inside the old engine shed at Boston Lodge. PRINCESS and her tender were given a lick of paint and spent time on display at Harbour station and Blaenau Ffestiniog before being refurbished and placed in the Museum at Porthmadog. As the least modified of the surviving England engines, she will remain as an exhibit. Her tender is now behind WELSH PONY, which stands on a plinth outside Harbour station awaiting a kindly millionaire!** *Sydney Leleux.*

19th October 1958. **Most of the restoration required on the railway has been done in-house, at Boston Lodge, but on occasions, items have been taken elsewhere for remedial attention. Wagons surviving after closure were all in poor condition and coal wagons were vital. The rebuild, using timber from condemned BR wagons, was carried out in Birmingham by volunteers from the FR Society Midland Group during the winter of 1958 and spring of 1959. Coal wagon No.19 was one to receive such attention, seen here in transit to its destination, shortly after being loaded at Harbour station, onto the back of H.Pountney Ltd.'s rather ancient looking lorry. It returned in time for the 1959 season. Note the presence of only one windscreen wiper on the lorry!** *Gerald Adams.*

16th May 1959. **One of the real delights of the FR is the unparalleled collection of views as the train climbs the route. Some of them are simply breathtaking and one of the most impressive structures on the line is the 62 ft. high Cei Mawr dry stone embankment. The railway has climbed to 225 ft. above sea level at this point, in a little over four miles from Porthmadog and something of the magnificence of the location can be seen in this view of TALIESIN hauling the first train of the day, bound for Tan-y-Bwlch. Fireman Jim Maxwell temporarily rests from his exertions to pose for the photographer, whilst the passengers in coach 23 peer out, wave and generally enjoy the early summer sun. Sadly, the growth of trees along the line has robbed both travellers and photographers of many of these views.** *Peter Gray.*

(opposite, top) 17th May 1959. **The following day and the sun still shines brightly. Driver David Rouse, wearing a broad grin, waits while his photograph is taken before restarting TALIESIN on its journey back to Porthmadog from Tan-y-Bwlch. The locomotive carries an amended maker's plate, bearing the message that it was rebuilt in 1956 at Boston Lodge. The young family, right, study the train, whilst the visitors to the left, seemingly unconcerned at joining the train, are either enjoying some refreshments from Bessie Jones' cafe, or are about to set out on a walk.** *Peter Gray.*

(opposite, bottom) 18th May 1959. **Caught in the act! As TALIESIN prepares to pass Minffordd crossing, driver David Rouse drops his lunch box onto the grass. Lottie Edwards, the crossing keeper seen right, will refill it for him and he will retrieve it on the next 'up' journey. Service, no doubt with a smile!** *Peter Gray.*

18th May 1959. **Later in the day and the sun has disappeared. Truly earning its keep, TALIESIN puts in the effort to climb the last stretch to Tan-y-Bwlch, rounding Whistling Curve with the 2.30 p.m. service from Portmadoc. Again, sadly, this view has been spoilt by tree growth.** *Peter Gray.*

5th March 1960. **Stock in Glan-y-mor yard, Boston Lodge. At preservation there were literally hundreds of slate wagons choking sidings throughout the railway. To clear space and realise cash, many were scrapped but a significant number survived as service vehicles. Those here are loaded with blocks of slate from one of the gate pillars at the Works entrance, which had to be demolished. Beneath the tarpaulins is carriage No.21, one of the Ashbury 'workmen's' carriages of 1896. A couple of years after this view, the carriage had to be condemned as it was beyond economic repair.** *David Rouse, M.J.S. coll.*

(above) *9th April 1960.* **Early in 1960, the A487 road out of Porthmadog was to be improved in connection with the planned transport of components to the newly-constructed Trawsfynydd nuclear power station. Just above Boston Lodge the railway ran beneath Rhiw Plas bridge, built to the normal loading gauge, tight width and with a pair of very sharp bends in the road. For a period there was a real threat that the road would simply be realigned without rebuilding the bridge, summarily severing the railway at this point and effectively ending the dream. Thankfully, some astute negotiating by legal minded supporters not only saved the railway but also brought about a complete rebuild of the bridge, to a far more sensible loading gauge. While the work was in progress, this temporary level crossing kept the road open.** *Gerald Adams.*

(right) *9th April 1960.* **The view through 180 degrees shows the reinforced concrete box, which will take the road overhead, rapidly taking shape around the railway, with here some of the shuttering used in the construction being removed. The road realignment meant this becoming almost a short tunnel. The new bridge formally opened on 1st June 1960.** *Gerald Adams.*

11th June 1960. **Whilst not exactly forgotten in all the hard work and celebrations of getting back to Tan-y-Bwlch, there was little time and no money to pay attention to the top end of the line at this time. Consequently, places such as Tanygrisiau, seen here, were left to their own devices and the hand of fate. A way has been forged for vehicular access to the houses, right, from the street below, whilst the old railway cottages on the far side of the station building have disappeared, a wall has been constructed blocking off the trackbed just past the old abandoned black car, and the skeleton of the power station is taking shape to the left. When compared with the 1990s view, the station site is barely recognisable.** *M.J.S. collection.*

29th June 1960. **The stalwart of services at this point, TALIESIN is seen once more, this time shunting stock at Harbour station, prior to working the 2.30 p.m. service up to Tan-y-Bwlch. In a delightful shot, coal is piled high in the bunkers and the engine exhaust matches the clouds. Note the proliferation of television aerials on Britannia Terrace, also the entrance to Britannia Foundry, right, doors wide open to let out some of the summer heat.** *Terry Gough.*

6th July 1960. A week on from the previous view and the 2.30 p.m. ex-Porthmadog is again seen behind TALIESIN, this time slowing for the stop at Minffordd station. The two Ashbury coaches, with their sagging bodies, lead the rake of externally very respectable stock. The entrance to the slope down to the British Railways station can just be seen to the left of TALIESIN, whilst to the right of the train, the 1926-installed crossover from 'down' to 'up' can be seen. *Terry Gough.*

(right) Summer 1960. Road and pedestrian access to the former South Snowdon wharf area at the bottom (southern) end of Harbour station was by of a level crossing. A track led to the wharf from the station approach and as can be seen from this specially prepared notice, there are no gates protecting the crossing from trains arriving at the station. This was a source of problem to the railway, as it interfered with the safe movement of locomotives running round their trains. When it was proposed to use the wharf to land materials for the building of Trawsfynydd power station, the opportunity was taken, in 1964, to route a new road around the headshunt by the water tower. This road is still in use, but now to serve the holiday flats that were built on the wharf a few years later. *Arthur Mace, Milepost 92½ collection.*

September 1960. The caption given to this shot by the photographer states, "The last original coach awaiting restoration in Boston Lodge old carriage shed." The coach is No.16 and the location is the old Joiners' Shop. Both look in need of remedial attention and it could be a question of which do you start first! The coach is one of the two 1872-vintage bogie coaches built by Brown, Marshalls to Charles Spooner's specification, both of which have thankfully survived. The scene remained much the same until 1962, when No.16 became the subject of a variety of homework projects by volunteers. The complete rebuild took eight years! The Joiners' Shop was not so lucky. As soon as No.16 was removed, the building was pulled down by MOELWYN - and not much effort was needed! *Gerald Adams.*

63

(above) 22nd April 1961. **FR Society AGM day and an historic date in the annals of the restored FR - the first re-appearance of two double-Fairlies at Harbour station. Newly-restored MERDDIN EMRYS negotiates the station trackwork, cabless in this dull, damp weather! To the left, TALIESIN has been renamed for the new season and stands at the head of the stock for the morning's first train in the new guise of EARL OF MERIONETH. Smoke and steam cover the station yard in the inclement conditions, putting a dampener on what should have been a celebration.** *Gerald Adams.*

(left) 22nd April 1961. **There was some concern about the reliability of MERDDIN EMRYS on his first day back in service, so the AGM train was run double-headed. Having safely reached Tan-y-Bwlch, MERDDIN EMRYS had to clear the top points, to allow EARL OF MERIONETH to run-round the train. Here perched precariously close to the unfenced Creuau Bank, which the locomotive has just crossed in this view looking back towards the station site, FR Society members have followed and are seen taking a keen interest in its restored persona.** *Gerald Adams.*

Chapter Three: 1961 - 1971.

1961 was a year of further consolidation, building on the previous year's success. PRINCE was due for a boiler examination - already five years since his return to duty! - and was to be fitted with new cylinders. MERDDIN EMRYS was making painfully slow progress since that earlier steaming, but at least began to look more like a whole locomotive once more and, thankfully, TALIESIN was still functioning without problem. Elsewhere, the Simplex had been converted to diesel propulsion, by virtue of a Gardner 4LK engine and its first outing in this mode was on 14th April. A week later and MERDDIN once more moved under its own steam.

The day of the 1961 FRS Annual General Meeting - 22th April - saw two double-Fairlies together in Harbour station for the first time for nearly thirty years, with MERDDIN EMRYS (formally entering service in July) double-heading a train to Tan-y-Bwlch with TALIESIN, now re-christened EARL OF MERIONETH.

Visitor numbers fluctuated greatly in the second-half of the season - something that would be experienced more than once in the years that followed - but overall, the railway held its own and even showed a slight increase in patronage, despite not having a TV fillip that year. The loop at Penrhyn was used for the first time as a passing loop, giving greater flexibility in operations; and Harbour station's coal stage was moved to sit, more conveniently, by the water tower.

By comparison, 1962 was an *annus horribilis* and a potential disaster for the railway, had it not been for rescue from an outside source.

Matters started well enough, with, at Easter, the first nine-coach train since restoration being hauled by the uncommon combination of MERDDIN EMRYS - still without cab - and MOELWYN, but the railway was running with its fingers crossed. PRINCE had not returned to duty and EARL OF MERIONETH was also out of action, for its five year inspection and awaiting retubing. With passenger numbers pushing the railway to the limit on many occasions, Allan Garraway was to comment in the Society's magazine, "It has, without doubt, been the most hectic operating season since the Simplex struggled across the Cob with two coaches back in 1955"! On the stock front, there was a constant battle to keep existing coaching stock running and to construct new additions, such as the ex-Lynton & Barnstaple No.14. Several had wooden underframes and were suffering the effects of age; not surprising when such as No.11 were around 90 years old!

EARL OF MERIONETH returned to traffic on 23rd June, but immediately MERDDIN EMRYS was taken out of service for attention. They then did a swap, but MERDDIN's condition gave cause for concern and the engine was withdrawn on 4th July, just four days before the peak season. Much 'burning of midnight oil' brought the EARL back to unplanned Top Link duties. PRINCE was close to completion, but even with that engine working full-time, the railway would still be in a potentially parlous situation. Salvation was to come

from Penrhyn Quarry at Bethesda, near Bangor, where operations were rapidly coming to a close.

Preliminary discussions had already taken place between Penrhyn and FR, with a view to the latter purchasing locomotives on closure, but matters were brought forward and 0-4-0ST LINDA was hired for the summer. She arrived on the FR on Saturday, 14th July, steamed the following day and immediately sent out with a six-coach train on test! Other than one or two relatively minor considerations, she was to prove a justification of expectations. So, on 15th July, the railway nominally had three engines in steam - the first time for many years.

Outwardly, services were run without further hitch for the rest of the summer, but like a swan paddling furiously whilst outwardly serene, there were many anxious moments behind the scenes!

August saw the first outing with the newly-constructed ex-L&B coach No.14 and a run through Garnedd Tunnel, north of Tan-y-Bwlch, which proved - to everyone's relief! - that clearance calculations had been correct. Meanwhile, much work had been undertaken at both Boston Lodge Works and the old engine shed, some at the former forced on the railway by the imminent collapse of the Joiner's Shop! At the top end of the line, at Blaenau Ffestiniog ex-LMS station, work was in full swing on the construction of the new road to Tanygrisiau, obliterating the original FR tracks into the town, except for the single line between Duffws and the former LMS yard, which still clung to a perilous existence until this year. 1962 ended with over 114,000 passenger journeys recorded.

1963 marked the Centenary of steam operation and the railway was not about to pass up the opportunity of publicly celebrating. The main event in the early part of the season was Press Day on 22nd May, when not only was PRINCE, then very nearly a grand old man of 100 years, the star attraction, but a renaissance of horse-drawn operation from the pre-1863 days was enacted, utilising horses which were still being used in heavy haulage at the Nantlle Railway. Ten days later, a new station was added to the line. Plas Halt, overlooking the grounds of Plas Tan-y-Bwlch, once the stately home of the Oakeley family, was opened by the then owners, Mr & Mrs Bibby. A request stop, it saw little use initially, but over the years, since the house was taken over by the Snowdonia National Park Authority as a study centre, it has become far more popular, (although not necessarily with the locomotive crews of 'Up' trains!).

By this time, LINDA had been fitted with wooden-framed wagon No.38 - once PRINCESS' tender - and with a vacuum ejector. On the timetable front, an innovation was the running of the 3.00 p.m. departure from Harbour non-stop to Tan-y-Bwlch, complete with curved 'Y Cymro' (The Welshman) headboard. During the season more journey records were broken, leading to some juggling of the rostered motive power.

10th August saw the completion and formal opening, by Her Majesty The Queen, of the hydro-electric scheme and power station at Tanygrisiau, and on the previous day the FR stationed PRINCE on the Minffordd mineral sidings, in sight of the Royal Train as it passed by on the Cambrian line. The one good thing to come out of this project, was a quantity of rail, fishplates and chairs donated to the FR by CEGB - and, in hindsight, it is probably a blessing in disguise to have the

5th August 1961. **A quiet scene at Harbour station, between trains; the highly unusual and somewhat complicated three-way point by the water tower is prominent in the foreground. Whilst serving the old railway well enough, the arrangement did not suit the requirements of the developing FR in the 1960s and after the realignment of the road to the old wharf site in 1964, this pointwork was altered. The arrangement initially went to Boston Lodge, before subsequently being transferred to Minffordd yard. The crossing can be seen here, running left to right, past the young boy and over some strategically placed sleepers between the rails. Note the old water tower still serving the railway, with point indicator signal and coaling platform made from old sleepers.** *F.C.Lemanquis, Milepost 92½ collection.*

railway operating on its new elevation into Tanygrisiau station.

The year ended as another record for passenger journeys and with the arrival of a second Hunslet locomotive from Penrhyn - BLANCHE. Sister to LINDA, she arrived by low-loader on 17th December.

One of the first jobs of 1964, on the ground, was the replacement of the ancient three-way stub point by the water tower at Harbour station, by more traditional layout, with the stub going to Glan-y-Mor yard at Boston Lodge. The level crossing to the old South Snowdon wharf was still extant at this time, but this was removed within weeks.

During April, the Royal Engineers undertook a training exercise on the railway and began erecting the steel frame of a second-hand building, acquired from Leeds, for an extension to the carriage shed at Boston Lodge. Also in April, LINDA appeared for the new season with a reprofiled cab and a new tender.

By this time, some initial thoughts on a route around the power station reservoir at Tanygrisiau were revealed. Three schemes had been mooted, with the favourite being to the east of the reservoir, the opposite side to that which was finally utilised.

Over the previous couple of years, a mixture of increased track mileage, peak passenger loading and projected growth, coupled with the inherent problem of operating with ancient stock, revealed the need for new coaching stock. The decision taken to build in-house, to the general outline of No.14, led to initial bodywork of what was to become No.24 being constructed at Birkenhead and moved to the FR in early March for further work. Featuring First and Third Class accommodation, it made its appearance in June, but bogie problems on curves gave some early cause for concern. Also in June, on the 24th, BLANCHE made her first trip up the line, without any heartaches and she then entered the full-time roster, usually hauling the 10.30 a.m. and 3.00 p.m. trains. Meanwhile, with an eye to future requirements, the layout at Tan-y-Bwlch was reorganised and the site generally tidied up; and in October the bodywork of what was to become Observation car No.100 was received.

During the winter of 1964/5, a completely new tender was fabricated for BLANCHE, of different design to that attached to LINDA; it incorporated a tender cab giving far

5th August 1961. As has been seen earlier in this book, the famous BR top-link driver Bill Hoole was a very early employee of the fledgling preserved FR and a tremendous asset to the railway. We therefore make no excuses for including this superb portrait of him in working clothes, standing by **EARL OF MERIONETH** at Tan-y-Bwlch. Though much smaller than his BR charges - and certainly travelling at much lower speeds! - he nonetheless took his FR locomotive duties very seriously. Sadly he suffered two strokes in 1967 and although continuing to take a keen interest in the FR, he played no further active part. He died in 1979; his passing greatly mourned. *F.C.Lemanquis, Milepost 92½ collection.*

5th August 1961. **Whilst literally thousands of people have taken photographs of Harbour station over the years, very few have considered this view. Taken from across the harbour, the delightful selection of period cars stand in a very open space outside the station buildings. On the site of old slate wharf sidings, the proliferation of cars over succeeding years has led to a much stricter control of parking and, in the 1990s, even charging for it.** *F.C.Lemanquis, Milepost 92½ collection.*

greater protection for the crew, especially when running downhill, tender-first in inclement weather. But perhaps the most far-reaching occasion was at Dduallt on 1st January. Whatever way forward was taken to Tanygrisiau, a 'deviation' was planned at Dduallt and this having been decided upon, the first sod was cut - seemingly in the middle of nowhere! Work would continue throughout the year, with various groups working at different points and achieving much progress.

On 24th May 1965, the Observation Car, with due ceremony, was handed over for operation, entering routine traffic the following day. Containing ten upholstered, pedestal-mounted swivel-chairs, it proved to be a great attraction. For AGM day, PALMERSTON, one of the original FR locomotives, that had stood unloved in Glan-y-Mor yard for many years, was somewhat dubiously painted in pink paint and rechristened HAROLD WILSON - from one Prime Minister to another! About this time, also, it was reported that in the ten years since 1955, with the exception of three or four isolated sections, all 15,000 or so sleepers between Portmadoc and Tan-y-Bwlch had been replaced! With journeys recording 150,000 for the first time and revenue up, it was a satisfactory year.

Before the 1966 season began, an arrival at Portmadoc made for an interesting comparison with FR stock. On 23rd March, the world's first Garratt, K1, built at Beyer Peacock's Gorton Foundry, Manchester in 1909, was delivered to Harbour station, having been bought by the FR on the closure of the Gorton establishment. It was placed on display at Harbour and drew attention from many hundreds over the next few years.

Elsewhere, digging and blasting at Dduallt continued, with progress at many points, but otherwise, progress of a different sort saw the first season for many without a double-Fairlie in operation. MERDDIN EMRYS, slightly 'sick', languished in Boston Lodge, only available for emergencies, until two weeks from the end of August. However, traffic receipts and the number of passengers carried increased again, despite the problems and the season ended with journeys approaching 174,000. How much longer could this continue?

Looking ahead to future developments, 1967 dawned with Permanent Way work concentrating on track relaying northwards from Tan-y-Bwlch towards Dduallt, with the stretch to Coed-y-Bleddiau virtually completed. This done, and with the final 200 lengths to Dduallt being in worse condition than recent stretches, focus moved back to Harbour station, where the platform was re-laid and the pointwork on the approach from the Cob moved further out towards Boston Lodge, to give greater operational flexibility for present and future.

To the relief of many, EARL OF MERIONETH returned to traffic at Easter, double-heading a train with BLANCHE. Certain attention had then to be given to the locomotive to cure steam leakages, but the ensuing weeks did see a full return to traffic.

During the year the railway was obviously still doing things right, as journeys again showed a record figure, this time exceeding 200,000. On 16th October, another locomotive arrived on the railway, one that would further ease any likely motive power problems. In 1964, John Ransom had bought an ex-World War 1 US ALCO 2-6-2T and after storage in London, he donated it in 1967 to the FR. The cab outline was outside of the FR loading gauge and, therefore, for its first run out on 4th November, amendments had to be made. These were temporary, before a more permanent outline was settled on - permanent, that is, until the 1980s, when a further redesign took place.

Meanwhile, work continued in getting the trackwork into proper shape for the push to Dduallt. Basic relaying was complete by late October, with the exception of Garnedd Tunnel and Dduallt station site. The sad news, however, was Bill Hoole suffering two strokes early in the year. Although he would revisit the FR, he was never to work on the railway again. Notice was also given that Will and Bessie Jones were to retire in 1968 - Tan-y-Bwlch would not be the same without them!

The major event of 1968 was undoubtedly the return of the railway to Dduallt, on 6th April. Despite restrictions on travel placed on the volunteers following the national outbreak of foot-and-mouth disease, trains were able to reach the new terminus, but as the run-round facilities had not been completed passengers were not allowed to detrain. The novelty of the extension obviously worked its magic, however, with traffic up by over 50% in the first month! The loop was finally commissioned on 20th May, but prior to this, the initial routine was for PRINCE to 'run light' to Dduallt before the first 'Up' train, after which 'Up' locomotives came off at Dduallt and worked the following 'Down' train, turn and turn about. As the summer wore on, traffic showed no signs of lessening and the Operating Department were hard pushed to keep services running. On 31st July and in August, 13 trains were run for

(right) 19th August 1961. **In the same way as the previous photograph is a different view of the railway, these two shots evidence a wider vision. Whilst most photograph the trains, relatively few bother with the signalling and even fewer in the early days of restoration.** *(top)* **Seen at Penrhyn, we have a 2'3" high disc signal capstan, the disc being 10" in diameter and the frame 2' across. All stations were protected by Up and Down Disc signals, operated by wires from capstans. The miniature disc was a repeater for the full-size item, which was usually out of sight of the capstan. This example stood just above the crossing at Penrhyn, where it could be conveniently operated in conjunction with the crossing signals** *(bottom).* **This type of signal was used both as a point indicator and to protect the level crossings at Penrhyn and both Yard entry road and Quarry Lane crossing at Minffordd. The top rotated, presenting the arm and a lamp in the disc when at 'Danger'.** *both Sydney Leleux.*

21st August 1961. **When the CEGB begin constructing their power station at Tanygrisiau, they carved an approach road straight across the trackbed at the end of the station. The effect of this can be seen here, with the station buildings defying all, with a wall constructed from them to the rockface, across the old formation. When the railway was planning its re-entry to Tanygrisiau, the need to pass the power station lake meant a higher elevation was required and this, in turn, caused the blasting of some of the rock on the left, to give access to the new tracks.** *Sydney Leleux.*

the first time. All this, sometimes frantic, activity took the journeys tally to just short of 300,000.

Into 1969, the Prince of Wales' Investiture Year, and plans were being made to add a pony truck to both LINDA and BLANCHE, to make them 2-4-0s and to give greater stability. The axles from the trailing bogie of the former Welsh Highland's MOEL TRYFAN were used for this purpose.

Out on the line, the water tank at Tan-y-Bwlch again had to be replaced and this time the opportunity was taken to increase the holding capacity by installing a 3500-gallon ex-road tanker on 12th May; this was followed six days later by a very public launch of the Coed Llyn Mair Nature Trail at Tan-y-Bwlch, making a useful adjunct to the existing appeal at the site, along with the new cafe. Thinking much further ahead, to publicise the 'Building Back To Blaenau' plans/campaign, PRINCESS was put on display outside the Stesion Fain in June, where she was visited by Prince Charles.

By the end of the summer, nearly a mile of the 'Deviation' formation was virtually complete. Though this may not sound very much, after nearly five years work, such was the isolated nature of Dduallt with its attendant logistical problems, the hardness of the rock and the work being almost entirely by hand by the volunteers, that it was a truly remarkable achievement. Work was also going on at Penrhyn, where the station was planned to be converted to a volunteer hostel for the 1970 season. The year ended with journey levels again exceeding previous records and consideration being given to the possibility of a Tan-y-Bwlch-Dduallt shuttle.

Sadly, 1970 was not to see Penrhyn hostel completed in time, but much needed work continued, preparing to give an eventual home to visiting volunteers. During October, in answer to the recurring fire-risk inherent with coal-fired locomotives and trees, LINDA, now running as a 2-4-0, was converted at Boston lodge to oil-firing. This gave other practical operating benefits, but in the short term made for a learning curve for footplate crews.

At the 'Deviation' site a few yards of the new formation were being used by locomotives for running-round and temporary tracks had been laid enabling works vehicles to be parked here, and it appeared that the 'western' side of the

power station reservoir had been decided on as the way forward. At Tan-y-Bwlch fencing was erected to segregate trains and public. This had involved pre-fabricating and erecting 526 ft. of fence, including four gates. This station also saw benefits from the newly-introduced shuttle service, both in traffic returns and in cafe/shop sales. 'Father Christmas' specials ran on 19/20th December and their success helped the year to end with another record journey tally, this time exceeding 350,000.

Although controversial, the decision to convert LINDA to oil-firing was vindicated by her performances and the decision was taken at the beginning of the year to similarly convert both BLANCHE and MOUNTAINEER, as soon as the necessary work could fitted into Boston Lodge's programme. Out on the line, a new footbridge at Tan-y-Bwlch was erected, and Penrhyn Hostel finally opened late in 1971. Initially only to organised groups, at 25p per person per night, it nevertheless gave both a much needed boost to facilities and incredible value for money.

On a less satisfactory note, the result of the Lands Tribunal deliberations over compensation for the loss of the route to Tanygrisiau awarded the railway only loss of profits, rather than reinstatement costs, i.e. £65,000 in place of the £153,000 claimed! This did, however, focus minds on the future and brought a determination to proceed to Blaenau Ffestiniog at all possible speed. Estimated Time of Arrival was 1978, but this proved a little optimistic, despite the first (trial) train crossing Rhoslyn bridge at Dduallt on 1st July and great strides being made on the great march northwards.

There were comments that the number and age of volunteers were moving in the wrong direction. Nearly thirty years later, the same comments were repeated looking into the next Millennium, but the FR has proved it can inspire sufficient to achieve wondrous things. On the ground, services continued to be well patronised and the 'novelty' of Dduallt had not worn off. There was a general air of satisfaction at what had been achieved in just over 15 years and an excitement about the future. As the Society's Annual Report put it, "The splendid thing about the present moment is that it is all future." - to 1972 and beyond.

29th August 1961. After the railway closed in August 1946, the lines linking the quarries above Duffws with the GWR and LMS stations were leased for them to preserve their outlets via the standard gauge. This at least gave the railway a small income and, for nearly twenty years, kept the rails from being looted for scrap. The former Glan-y-Pwll engine shed, seen in the centre of this view, had already been let to a timber merchant, who installed the crane. After this use finished, there was a fire, evidence of which can just be seen on the exposed roof timbers, which subsequently collapsed. Later, some of the internal wall of the shed also collapsed, but happily, some of the original building survived for the preservationists to incorporate it into the restored structure. The 1899 route to Dinas swung to the left here, on the bank of Afon Barlwydd, past the small van standing on the old trackbed. *Sydney Leleux.*

29th August 1961. At this time, the route into Blaenau Ffestiniog was still extant, but will only have a further year to live, before the Tanygrisiau road realignment intervened. This is the point seen in the picture on page 12, showing PRINCESS in January 1946, just before closure. As can be seen, the ensuing fifteen years have seen little change, with the right-hand tracks still in use by the quarries. *Sydney Leleux.*

29th August 1961. A last look at the old Central station in Blaenau Ffestiniog. The FR's line to Duffws runs in from the left, with a line to the slate sidings crossing the standard gauge tracks in the foreground on an uncommon diamond formation. The ex-GWR goods shed dominates the mid-distance, with the joint station and the white building of the Queen's Hotel to the left. At this point, the standard gauge was merely a headshunt, but obviously out of use, with sleepers and rocks placed across it. The FR's tracks were still in use, until 1962, by Oakeley Quarry, for transhipment from Duffws to the old LMS site. With all services to the GWR station having ceased on 30th January 1961, this site was very soon to become a railway 'ghost town'. *Sydney Leleux.*

(above) 15th July 1962. In 1962, the FR was finding itself acutely short of available motive power and after an approach to Penrhyn Quarries, 0-4-0ST LINDA was brought to the railway on 14th July. Built in 1893 by Hunslet, with 2'1" driving wheels, the locomotive had become surplus at the quarry, as operations between the quarry near Bethesda and Port Penrhyn ceased in July 1962. Initially coming to the FR on loan, LINDA never went away! In 'quarry condition', she is seen here just a few hours after arrival, on her first outing arriving at Minffordd. David Rouse observes proceedings from the coach balcony, whilst Paul Dukes - Boston Lodge supremo - acts as fireman. As seen, she began work without a tender, but was fairly quickly coupled to wagon No.38, formerly the tender of PRINCESS. Subsequently, she was paired on a permanent basis with a especially modified tender from WELSH PONY. *M.J.S. collection.*

(left) 5th September 1962 An occasion now into the annals of the FR as 'Linda's Leap'! More than thirty years afterwards, this potentially catastrophic event is one that many would rather forget. Approaching the delightfully named Squirrel Crossing, LINDA apparently decided to go for a walk in the woods! Without a tender, she was double-heading with PRINCE on a service train; the bouncing motion of the two 0-4-0 tank engines and what was later found to be a seized axlebox on the ex-Penrhyn locomotive, combined to produce the result seen here. Fortunately, the accident, whilst spectacular, caused no injuries to passengers nor serious damage to either engine. In the lower view, Works Foreman Paul Dukes is supervising the 'packing and jacking' procedure, to restore LINDA to the rails. Once back in the Works, the slight damage to eccentrics repaired and the axlebox problem identified, she was back at work in a matter of days. *both M.J.S.collection.*

(above) 14th September 1962. Volunteers hard at work. After much clearance around Glan-y-mor yard at Boston Lodge, seven intrepid souls put in valuable man hours re-laying track. The original carriage shed stands in the lee of the cliff face, still in fair condition. Two years on from this view, the yard was in full use and an extension to the shed was being put together. In the background, the ex-Harrogate Gas Works Peckett locomotive can be seen. *M.J.S.collection.*

(centre) January 1963. Winter in North Wales can be bitterly cold and especially when working outdoors. Frost can just be seen on the sleepers, on what looks to be newly-laid track, just above the 5-mile point at Cutting Budr and the two volunteers burn sleepers to release rail chairs as well as wielding their mattocks, in an attempt to keep warm. Gloves, berets and greatcoat are the order of the day. A pile of fishplates and sundry ironwork is piled by the line, awaiting re-use elsewhere. *M.J.S.collection.*

22nd May 1963. To celebrate one hundred years of steam operation on the Festiniog Railway, special events were put on during 1963, including a symbolic re-creation of the original horse-drawn mode of transport. On Press Day, having just completed a demonstration 'haul', horse and minder stand in harbour station for their photograph, the chains just having been released from the wagon behind, whilst a large crowd, including some in period costume, pays attention to the equally-aged PRINCE in the background. *M.J.S. collection.*

(left) 19th August 1963. As part of the celebrations, ancient four-wheeled coaches were 'spruced up'. Right to left, Nos.5 (compartment), 6 (open) and 8 (quarrymen's) stand in Harbour station yard, quite possibly in the best external condition that they had been in for many a year! *Sydney Leleux.*

(centre) 19th August 1963. The aforementioned road realignments at Blaenau Ffestiniog dramatically altered the railway topography near to the ex-LMS station. A comparison with the middle picture on page 71 will show just how much. The old FR tracks still just cling to their pathway to the right, and the retaining wall is common to the two views, but the old 'main line' has been obliterated by the construction of this new bridge, which will eventually facilitate standard gauge tracks running from here to the old Central station for the first time. The 1956-constructed BR station on the LMS site, can be seen through the left-hand arch. *Sydney Leleux.*

(bottom) 19th August 1963. Just a couple of hundred yards closer to Blaenau town centre and the old GWR headshunt has been bulldozed out of existence. The original FR route still clings to its alignment, right, but this will be the path of the BR tracks when the infrastructure works have been completed, with the new FR tracks running to the left, on the alignment holding the crane here. The BR line was required for running nuclear waste trains through to Trawsfynydd, on the old Blaenau-Bala line. New fencing will be put in by the houses, once the replacement Picton bridge, pictured in front of the crane, is fully in use. *Sydney Leleux.*

21st August 1963. As previously mentioned, soon after LINDA's arrival on the FR, she was temporarily paired with the tender previously coupled to PRINCESS. The somewhat incongruous pairing is seen with Allan Garraway in charge at Harbour station, whilst backing into the platform road. A Heath Robinson arrangement for water from a tender reservoir has made fortuitous use of some rusted platework. In the background, Britannia Foundry still operates, but will close within two years. At one time it cast items for the railway and gave much needed employment in the town. Its place was eventually taken by a new building of Inland Revenue offices! *Sydney Leleux.*

21st August 1963. Running any railway requires a whole raft of different stock, not just locomotives, coaches and wagons. The FR has been no exception. Two of the more esoteric items, a plate bender and a horse dandy, (the latter having been used as a coal wagon in its later years), stand in the yard at Boston Lodge, obviously not in every day use. The legend 'scrap' can just be seen on the dandy; fortunately, this was saved and is now in the Museum at Porthmadog. The plate bending rolls, mounted on an old slate wagon, are still in regular use at Boston Lodge. *Sydney Leleux.*

21st August 1963. Until WW1, locomotives were turned at the end of each trip on tables at Glan-y-Pwll (Blaenau Ffestiniog) and Boston Lodge, where the table was just up the line from the engine shed and reached by a turn-out from the main line. After the railway closed, the tenant of No.3 cottage, Rev. Timothy Phillips, built his garage on the 22ft. deck of this latter turntable, the plan being that the car could be driven in, the table rotated and the car then driven out without the need to reverse. No three-point turns then needed! Sadly, in practice the extra weight of the garage and the difficulty of balancing the car made the scheme impractical. Both garage and hidden turntable are still in place. *Sydney Leleux.*

29th August 1963. **In this view of Old Dinas Junction and Barlwyd Bridge, just short of Glan-y-Pwll on the approach to Blaenau Ffestiniog, the position of three tracks can be seen. To the left, the trackbed of the Nidd-y-Gigfan quarry branch can clearly be seen swinging sharp left through the stone gate pillars; centre is the original single-track route to Dinas, now buried beneath the slate scree; whilst to the right is the remaining section of the pre-1946 operational FR, parallel tracks that ran to Glan-y-Pwll Junction, before splitting for Stesion Fain and, post-1899, to Dinas. In the right distance, the Oakeley Quarry viaduct can be seen, crossing the ex-LNWR/LMS tracks.** *Sidney Leleux.*

29th August 1963. **Through the photographs in this book, we have seen the gradual deterioration of Tanygrisiau station. By 1963 it is looking decidedly sad. The old goods shed still stands, but the station building itself has been reduced to mere stone pillars. All the trackwork has been lifted, but the small turntable by the shed is extant. Just above the low wall, right, can be seen the recently-built lighter coloured retaining wall for the approach road to the power station, built on the old FR trackbed.** *Sydney Leleux.*

13th July 1964. Like her sister LINDA, BLANCHE came from the Penrhyn quarries, being bought in 1963. Also like LINDA, BLANCHE was built by Hunslet in 1893 and was paired with the old tender from PRINCESS in her early days on the FR. Still as an 0-4-0ST, in Penrhyn livery and retaining the rear cab-sheet, but now fitted with vacuum brake, she stands in Harbour station, having just arrived with a train. Note that the connection from the tender has a far more professional appearance than when fitted to LINDA, and that the platework has been patched. The level crossing has gone, but that the roadway round the headshunt is still not fenced from the railway.

C.L.Caddy.

Summer 1964. Another view of BLANCHE, still with that tender, acting as shunting engine in the exchange sidings in Minffordd yard. The standard gauge 16 Ton steel-bodied coal wagon, on the siding from the Cambrian Coast line, makes an interesting comparison with the far more ancient slate wagon conversions being operated by the FR. The chute arrangement between standard and narrow gauge, is an interesting one, being designed to cope with coal and to sieve dirty ex-BR ballast. *H.Lawson Kerr; Peter Johnson collection.*

Summer 1965. Another photograph superbly displaying the scenic and aesthetic delights as the railway courses through the highly attractive North Wales countryside. Running with the Observation Car at the head of the rake, PRINCE slows for the Penrhyn road crossing, in hot summer sunshine. On the hill, to the left, is another view of the white house owned by Paul and Hilary Davies, both volunteers on the FR and fine B&B hosts. *Terry Gough.*

Summer 1965. Another view of the Observation Car seen behind PRINCE. Put into traffic in May 1965, No.100 was the first of a series of new vehicles built by the railway to cope with a steadily increasing traffic load. They make full use of the available loading gauge and were built to a profile that had been proved with the rebuild of the ex-Lynton & Barnstaple coach seen behind No.100 here. The 'Barns', as their impressive size soon led them to being dubbed, were all corridor connected and set the standard for future new coach build on the railway. As the new Millennium dawned, however, these vehicles were deemed beyond economic repair as they became due for overhaul, most having been rebuilt once already. Note that by this time, a wall has been built, left, to keep the public away from the track leading to the water tower. *Peter Johnson collection.*

24th August 1965. BLANCHE's regular driver, after she arrived on the FR, did not share the views of Sir Arthur Heywood and Manager Allan Garraway, that "a stout mackintosh is better for the driver than a cab" and his solution to the often indifferent weather in this part of Wales can be seen in the impressive new tender, complete with cab extension, fitted this year and prominent in this view. Note that the track layout has been altered, with the removal of the three-way point, and a fence has appeared separating the new road from the railway. *Alan Ashworth, M.J.S. collection.*

28th November 1965. With the flooding of the original route north of Moelwyn tunnel, in the power station scheme, a new route northwards from Dduallt was needed. The new line would have to gain considerable height, both to rise above the new lake and to pass the power station itself. The solution was ingenious and innovative and involved the construction of the first railway spiral in the British Isles. The works involved, soon known as the 'Deviation', were remarkable for being undertaken almost entirely by volunteers using techniques which would have been familiar to the navvies building the earliest railways. This involved major works, including blasting solid rock with dynamite to form a cutting on one part of the site and then using this rock to help build up embankments elsewhere. There were a number of sites and this is a view of Site 3, with volunteers manhandling a wagon of rock, building up the formation. *Gerald Adams.*

(centre) 30th April 1966. To coincide with the FR Society AGM in 1966, PALMERSTON, languishing in Glan-y-mor yard, Boston Lodge, was mysteriously repainted pink and named after the then incumbent of No.10 Downing Street. The 'powers that be' were 'not amused'; the full story of this prank is still known only to those involved! *Ray Misson.*

15th May 1966. Dduallt station site, with the original track on the left, heading towards the flooded Moelwyn tunnel. Meanwhile, construction of the 'Deviation' is gathering momentum, with tracks now swinging to the right, to start the spiral that will eventually take the railway over itself at the other end of the station site. A young family examines the old route, safe in the knowledge that no trains will be running that way. *Gerald Adams.*

15th May 1966. Another, more elevated view of Dduallt. The roof of Rhoslyn shines brightly in the sunshine, with the station site itself being the open stretch just to the left. Some of the new embankment construction can be seen above this, the new rock marching toward the eventual site of a new bridge crossing over the railway, in lighter tone to the surrounding terrain. The fact that Dduallt is isolated and unapproachable by road can be well seen from this vantage point. In the distance, the huge bulk of Trawsfynydd nuclear power station dominates the horizon. *Gerald Adams.*

15th July 1966. The history of K1, the world's first Garratt locomotive, with its twists and turns and near-miraculous salvation, has been told in other places, but part of its story involves the FR. Under the auspices of then FR Society Chairman, Bill Broadbent, K1 was bought by the railway when the Beyer, Peacock Works at Gorton in Manchester were closed, for £1000 purchase price and £400 travel costs. In March 1966, it arrived at Harbour station and was put back together on the old WHR spur, by the goods shed. Moving then to a siding in the yard, it became a focus for many cameras over the next few years, although its importance in locomotive design was probably unknown to a majority of visitors. It stands here in near-original black-lined livery. *John Clay.*

August 1966. Another shot showing the appeal of the FR. The massive 1830s-built 62ft. high Cei Mawr dry-stone embankment dwarfs BLANCHE and PRINCE as they climb across it, heading for Tan-y-Bwlch. The twelve-coach train is highly unusual, as is the double-heading and no doubt this was the result of some special event. Virtually all of the available coaching rolling stock is in evidence here. Sadly, as with so many other points on the railway around Tan-y-Bwlch, this view is no longer available, due to afforestation and the general growth in tree height. *J.Dobson, Peter Johnson collection.*

(page 84) September 1966. Once more the beauty of the railway and its environs is highlighted. On a delightful early autumn day BLANCHE approaches the 60-yd. Garnedd tunnel, the tightest loading gauge on the line, on the first stretch up from Tan-y-Bwlch, with Llyn Mair in the valley below. Some of the problems encountered by the 1830s navvies, when constructing the original line, can be imagined from this view of the railway clinging to the mountain side. *R.C.Riley.*

(this page) 6th April 1968. Re-opening to Dduallt had been advertised for the 1968 season, but work had been severely hampered during the early part of the year by the outbreak of foot-and-mouth disease. To have brought volunteers from other parts of the country with all the attendant risks of contamination, would have been unforgivable. The work outstanding was completion of the loop, as can be seen in this view of the first train of the season. Until the loop was finished, PRINCE ran up the line and into the siding on the right before the first train of the day. When this arrived, he came out, as seen here, coupled to the bottom end and took the train down again. Throughout the day, the train engine then waited in the siding until the next arrival, when the process was repeated. *R.G.Roscoe, FR Archives.*

(page 86) Spring 1969. 1967 saw the arrival on the FR of MOUNTAINEER. Originally built by the American Locomotive Co. in 1917, for service in war-torn France, it came to the railway as a donation from Society Director John Ransom. Although easily built for the '2ft.' gauge, the sheer bulk of the engine dwarfed the railway's rolling stock. This can be seen in this view at Minffordd, with the cab already altered to fit the restricted loading gauge as it prepares to haul its train to Porthmadog. Within a couple of years the cab would be altered yet again. Norman Kneale.

(this page) Spring 1970. Disappearing into Boston Lodge Works at the end of the 1966 season, MERDDIN EMRYS eventually re-appeared looking very different. Gone were the attractive and graceful rounded lines and in their place, were blunt D-shaped smokebox saddle, denuded cab sides, square tanks and parallel boiler. Newly finished, it is time to brave the public gaze. Compared to it's earlier - and, thankfully, later - shape, this was not an improvement. Note the sale notice on Britannia Foundry - some five years after closure. Jon Marsh.

(above) Spring 1970. **Put to work, the motion is in need of some oil, during a stop at Minffordd. The gentleman to the right stares incredulously at the lines of MERDDIN EMRYS, whilst a young lady, left, giggles - perhaps she is not impressed with the alterations!** *Norman Kneale.*

(opposite) 29th May 1970. **The more classic lines originally worn by MERDDIN EMRYS and still gracing EARL OF MERIONETH, seen here at the water tower in Harbour station, are aesthetically far more pleasing than those of the last two views of MERDDIN, a fact reinforced in this angle. Preparing to run round its train, the EARL has received a refill of coal from the ample supply of good quality lumps, right. Note the wicker basket to load the bunkers.** *R.E.Ruffell, Peter Johnson collection.*

August 1970. A scene of delightful rural quality, at Penrhyn. MOUNTAINEER leaves the station with the first train of the day, probably the 10.30 a.m. ex-Porthmadog, bound for Dduallt, in an uneven race with an elderly tractor, which is still running uphill, whilst MOUNTAINEER is much closer to level. Dduallt station had rejoined the rest of the FR in 1968, becoming the northern terminus for the next nine years, as volunteers built the 'Deviation' to reach Tanygrisiau once more. *John Hunt.*

September 1970. Tunnel Mess, seen here at the far end of the line, by Moelwyn tunnel's southern portal, was already a second-hand Terrapin building when reclaimed for further use, between 1967 and 1979, by the volunteer navvies building 'The Deviation'. The curious structure on top was a water tank, the supply for which came from behind a dam built in the old 730-yd. Moelwyn tunnel. The tracks form the 1842 'direct' route north, replacing the earlier, temporary, method of crossing the rocky outcrop. This involved a pair of inclines, one of which can be seen running away to the left. *Jon Marsh.*

(above) September 1970. As this part of the railway 'slept', the trackbed turned green and the houses stood sentinel, the occupants getting on with business, giving little or no thought to the railway. This is the view north, as the railway squeezes between housing on its way out of Tanygrisiau, heading for the 'slate dominated' run to Blaenau Ffestiniog and the terminus. *Jon Marsh.*

(right) March 1971. LINDA was converted to oil firing in 1970 and BLANCHE in 1971. On a very wet and dull early spring day, the former stands at the water tower in this altered condition. Driver and General Manager Allan Garraway was a firm believer in oilskins for enginemen, hence no back sheet on the cab. Pity the fireman on the 'down' journey!!! *Norman Kneale.*

(this page) Summer 1971. It is probable that many travellers do not give a second thought to the behind-the-scenes effort required in running a professional and successful railway. Many man hours, often by volunteers, are spent in effecting smooth operations and not least towards this, is the preparation and condition of the locomotives. Here EARL OF MERIONETH receives both coal and a clean at Boston Lodge, before duty. One by-product of coal operation is ash and some of the quantity and the associated disposal problem can be judged from the wagons in the foreground. *Jon Marsh.*

(page 93) Summer 1971. With the opening of Dduallt in 1968, Tan-y-Bwlch became a passing place for trains, rather than the terminus. Obviously, the previous facility of travellers/visitors wandering around the Tan-y-Bwlch site could not be countenanced with more than one train running and the solution was to build an island platform, first used on 27th May 1968, with access by footbridge. This latter was erected during the 1970/71 winter and gave photographers a whole new vantage point, as well as safeguarding the public. Fencing was erected to further enhance safety in 1969. Double Fairlies meet on a dull summer's day, as EARL OF MERIONETH, in its final season, working hard up the gradient into the station, arrives with an 'up' train, passing, right, MERDDIN EMRYS awaiting the road for the run to Porthmadog. *Jon Marsh.*

(left) Summer 1971. **The FR lives or dies by its success in attracting visitors. An important element in this is the family, especially those with young children. Get them hooked young and, hopefully, they will stay supporters for life. Whether this young is perhaps too early is uncertain, but in coach No.106, the view of the photographer's wife and daughter, Anne and Vicky, epitomises the welcome the railway is keen to give to all its visitors.** *Jon Marsh.*

(below) Summer 1971. **MOUNTAINEER initially arrived on the FR with a plain stovepipe chimney. However, in an attempt to overcome problems with sparks setting fire to the trees along the route south of Tan-y-Bwlch, it was fitted in 1971 with a spark-arrestor. The somewhat hideous contraption did nothing for the aesthetics of the locomotive, as can be seen in this view of it leaving Cei Mawr on a Porthmadog-Dduallt service. Note the addition of the FR's original locomotive** *Mountaineer's* **bell, and that the cab is still in initial FR shape. The bell was later removed, being merely cosmetic and an irrelevance from an operating standpoint.** *Jon Marsh.*

Winter 1971. **Now fully settled into oil-firing, LINDA receives some TLC in Boston Lodge yard. She is here running with the hideous grey aluminium-coloured chimney and smokebox.** *Norman Kneale.*

Winter 1971. **A scene that would not have looked out-of-place nearly one hundred years earlier. EARL OF MERIONETH stands at the top of the Long Shed at Boston Lodge, put into 'store' for the winter. All moving parts have been well greased, as well as the cylinder covers and smokebox door visible here, to prevent any deterioration in the damp winter weather and to ease eventual preparations for the next spring's services. There may have been dramatic technological progress over the last century, but some things never change! In fact, the locomotive never returned to service, being withdrawn for conservation as the last original Ffestiong Railway double-Fairlie. After years of inactivity, it was cosmetically restored in the late-1980s, going on long-term loan to the National Railway Museum at York in October 1988.** *Norman Kneale.*